"From its opening pages, Dai . . . . heart gazing at Jesus as my greatest need and greatest hope in the world. This book is gritty, powerful and rich with good news. I didn't realise just how much I needed to read it. Dai writes as one who knows what it means to hold on to hope through the inevitable dark seasons of life. I thought often of the words of 17th-century pastor Thomas Watson, who wrote, 'When God lays men upon their backs, then they look up to heaven.' That is exactly what Dai does through each and every chapter. Here you will find not only the light of biblical theology but also the warmth of pastoral tenderness and personal experience. No matter where you are in your walk with Jesus, this is a book that will, I am confident, put fuel in your tank and rekindle fire in your heart."

ADAM RAMSEY, Lead Pastor, Liberti Church, Gold Coast, Australia; Director, Acts 29 Asia Pacific; Author, *Truth on Fire* and *Faithfully Present*

"If you have come to the point of collapse, or you fear that you will soon fall or you dread that there is nothing left then Dai Hankey is writing for you. As well as for me. *Hopeward* is an honest, warm and kind book for Christians who are struggling to feel anything like hope. It is honest, warm and kind because that is how Dai writes, but more because he writes about Jesus. The deep and clear focus on how the Lord himself is all we need when we have nothing left will bring hope. This book will not bring you back to Christ, it will show how Christ comes to you, and brings you back to life."

JOHN HINDLEY, Pastor, BroadGrace Church, Norfolk; Author, *Serving without Sinking* and *Refreshed: Devotions for Your Time Away*

"Dai, in his characteristically honest, vulnerable and raw style has put together a much needed 'MOT' for all those on the narrow path. New follower of Christ or old war horse—this is for you. We all need to stop and recalibrate. If you're burned out, this is for you. If you're doing great right now, this is for you. Each chapter also has some pithy questions you can look at in small groups or with your mates. Read, reflect and get on the front foot of God's purposes for your life."

CARL BEECH, CEO, Edge Ministries

"Full of the fresh air of grace, this book is like gospel rehab for the weary. Short and simple (in the best sense of the word!), and yet full of honest, heartwarming and healing truth, reading this will do your heart good."

LINDA ALLCOCK, Author, *Deeper Still: Finding Clear Minds and Full Hearts through Biblical Meditation*

HOPEWARD

DAI HANKEY

Hopeward
© Dai Hankey, 2023.

Published by:
The Good Book Company

thegoodbook.com | thegoodbook.co.uk
thegoodbook.com.au | thegoodbook.co.nz | thegoodbook.co.in

ISBN: 9781784989088 | JOB-007284 | Printed in the United Kingdom

Design by Drew McCall

To Hodgey, Owens and Nick—
the finest of friends through the toughest of times!

CONTENTS

THE HOPEWARD TRAJECTORY

RUN >>

WALK >>

GROW >>

FEAST >>

ABIDE >>

RECEIVE >>

COME >>

WELCOME

I LAY IN A CRUMPLED HEAP
NOT STRONG, BUT WEAK
A PITIFUL MESS BUT BLESSED
TO COLLAPSE AT THE MASTER'S FEET.

This is a book for weary pilgrims, discouraged disciples, broken-hearted believers and faltering followers of Jesus.

It's a book for the deflated and defeated.

For the done-in and the burned out.

It's for people who secretly want to quit—or who have already.

It's a book for doubters and sceptics whose minds are a frenzy of unresolved questions; it's for fearful friends whose hearts are crippled with anxiety; it's for prodigals, rebels and wretches who know exactly why their faith is in tatters but are not sure if there's a way back.

It's a book for people who are holding it together but feel like the string is about to snap.

And it's for people who are well past breaking point already: who find themselves in a crumpled heap with nothing left to give and nowhere left to turn.

People like me.

The truth is that this book is written as much for myself as it is for anyone else. Or to put it another way: this is not a sermon—this is my story.

This is the testimony of a broken man who recently, and not for the first time, found himself down-and-out—a pitiful mess in deep distress. Please believe me when I say that I have had to navigate many dark days when I didn't know how to carry on. I felt like a spent force with a faith that barely flickered. The future was a terrifying fog of chaotic uncertainty.

Perhaps you can relate to some of that? Or maybe you're not there yet, but you can feel yourself slipping, sliding, slumping—and it's scaring you.

The reasons that drove me to that place of defeat are many and varied and will no doubt spill out in the pages that follow. But by God's grace I have lived to fight (and write) another day and it is my prayer that this book will help you to discover what, or rather *who*, pulled me through. The hero of this book is not me; it is my merciful Saviour—Jesus Christ. He saved (and continues to save) me and graciously put me on a hopeward pathway to recovery, restoration and renewal.

He can do the same for you too. So, if you're up for it, let's begin where I had to start: in a crumpled heap at the Master's feet...

1. COME TO JESUS

(He welcomes the weary)

MY TROUBLED SOUL WAS WEARY
MY HEART WAS COLD AND HEAVY
"COME, RECEIVE MY REST"
HE WHISPERED TO ME GENTLY.

*"Come to me, all who labour and are heavy laden,
and I will give you rest." (Jesus in Matthew 11:28)*

I've lost track of how many times over the years I've
preached these words of Jesus to weary souls, scribbled
them in cards for the burdened, and prayed them over the
broken-hearted. Surely there are no sweeter words than
these, spoken by the gentlest and most loving person
who ever walked the earth—the Lord Jesus Christ. They
have served me well as I have sought to encourage others
through life's darkest seasons, both as a pastor and a friend.

Yet if I'm honest, for most of my Christian life they were
words that were great for other people—but not so much
for me.

I was always more excited by some of Jesus' other com-
mands and exhortations. For example, his invitation to
"Follow me" (Mark 2:14), given to working-class fishermen

and crooked tax collectors, was an offer that I could get on board with. It had a ring of adventure and divine purpose to it which really appealed to an adrenaline junkie like me. So when Jesus held that offer out to me as a good-for-nothing 15-year-old, I grabbed it with both hands.

I later learned that there was also a significant cost to following Jesus: "If anyone would come after me, let him deny himself and take up his cross and follow me" (Mark 8:34). Now Jesus was not just calling me to follow him but to carry a cross while I did. Wow! This was the next level. Far from daunting me, this verse inspired me even more—it smacked of passionate sacrifice, and I'd seen enough movies to know that sacrifice was the greatest expression of love and also the best way to die. "Yeah, sign me up for adventure and sacrifice for King Jesus," I thought. "Let's go!"

And there was more...

As my love for Jesus deepened, I discovered what my "laid down" life should look like. I realised that following him required more than simply reading epic promises in my Bible and pouring my guts out in prayer (though those are great things to do). Prior to heading back to heaven, Jesus had left specific instructions for his people to obey:

> *Go ... and make disciples of all nations, baptising them in the name of the Father and of the Son and of the Holy Spirit, teaching them to observe all that I have commanded you. And behold, I am with you always, to the end of the age. (Matthew 28:19-20)*

More than mere sacrificial adventure, Jesus was sending us on a mission. And what a mission—a search and rescue operation that was global in scope and eternal in significance. And even better (for a gobby so-and-so like me) it involved opening my big mouth and telling other people about the same love that had transformed my life. Perfect!

Follow me on an adventure worth giving your life for. ✓

Go and change the world in my name. ✓

Come to me, all you who are weary and burdened. ✗

Nah, I didn't need verses like that last one—they were for weak Christians, not for the strong, sorted, spiritually courageous types like me.

I was happy to "go" for Jesus, but I really didn't feel the need to "come" to him.

Proverbs 16:18 says, "Pride goes before destruction, and a haughty spirit before a fall".

I was such a proud fool!

A CRUMPLED HEAP

I can't really put my finger on exactly what happened or why...

Maybe it was the demands of ministry. My family and I had been living and serving for two decades in some of the toughest communities in South Wales. Perhaps it was an accumulation of the countless soul-crushing discouragements, disappointments, betrayals and rejection we had faced.

Maybe it was physical. Had the many years of destroying my body on a skateboard (and the multiple surgeries that followed) finally caught up with me?

Maybe it was emotional. Perhaps I had never really grieved properly after Mam died, or fully come to terms with the emotional fallout of my wife's recent bout of poor mental health.

Maybe it was spiritual. Preaching the gospel, planting churches and fighting modern slavery involve a level of brutal spiritual warfare that is easy to underestimate.

Maybe I'd been mugged by middle age.

Or maybe, like for so many other people, it was lockdown.

Like I said, I don't really know. It could have been all of the above or none of it, but a time came towards the end of 2020 when I broke. Strong, cocky, courageous Dai lay flat on his back staring obsessively at a crack in the ceiling. I was deaf to my wife's voice, numb to her touch, oblivious to a world beyond my shattered self. Frantic thoughts were ricocheting around my mind—furious one minute, panicking the next. Blaming others. Hating myself. Trying to work out how to fix it. Then how to quit. How to correct the skid. Then how to crash as hard as I could. What to do next. What all this meant for my family.

Flip...

Would my family not just be better off without me?

My wife certainly deserves better...

My church could do so much better...

And Jesus gave me a job to do—

He told me to go...

... but I've literally got *nothing* left to give.

I'm empty.

I'm out.

It's over.

AT THE MASTER'S FEET

I am aware that my experience will not resonate with everyone reading this. Some of you will have equally extreme stories. Some even more so. Others, however, may have never found themselves in this place... yet. However, you often feel jaded and discouraged. Life feels like a relentless treadmill that just... won't... stop...

Whoever you are, and wherever you're at, it is my prayer that what you read in these pages will encourage you that a crumpled heap at the Master's feet is far from finished. I would even go so far as to say that it is only when we have come to Jesus and collapsed in exhaustion before him that we are able to start plumbing the true depths of his grace. The hymnwriter Annie Johnson Flint was right on the money when she wrote:

> *When we have exhausted our store of endurance,*
> *When our strength has failed ere the day is half done,*
> *When we reach the end of our hoarded resources,*
> *Our Father's full giving is only begun.*

His love has no limit;
His grace has no measure.
His pow'r has no boundary known unto men;
For out of His infinite riches in Jesus,
He giveth, and giveth, and giveth again.

At some point in the midst of my crumpling, God opened my eyes to a beautiful truth: that I was in very good company lying at the feet of Jesus. Indeed, the Gospels are full of men and women who found themselves in the exact same place:

- The leper knelt at Jesus' feet and was cleansed (Matthew 8:1-4).

- The demon-possessed man fell at Jesus' feet and was delivered (Mark 5:1-20).

- The sinful woman wept at Jesus' feet and was forgiven (Luke 7:36-50).

- Jairus bowed at Jesus' feet and his daughter was raised from death (Mark 5:21-43).

- The lame, blind, crippled and mute were laid at Jesus' feet and were all healed (Matthew 15:29-31).

- Mary sat at Jesus' feet and soaked up every wonderful word he spoke (Luke 10:39).

THE INVITATION

It was here, wrecked at the feet of Jesus, as God tenderly crushed the pride out of me, that I was able to hear this gracious invitation with fresh ears for myself:

*Come to me, all who labour and are heavy laden, and
I will give you rest. Take my yoke upon you, and learn
from me, for I am gentle and lowly in heart, and you
will find rest for your souls. For my yoke is easy, and
my burden is light. (Matthew 11:28-30)*

And I was glad to respond.

These words are now some of the sweetest words to me
in all of Scripture. They were strong, kind words that cut
through the chaos of my turbulent mind and whispered
grace and peace and hope to my weary soul when I really
needed them.

There is so much that can and has been written about
these words. (I would recommend Dane Ortlund's book
Gentle and Lowly if you'd like to dig deeper.) My purpose
in this chapter, however, is simply to introduce this invitation as the starting point of a hopeward journey that
this book is going to take us on. And there are three
things about this invitation that I particularly want us
to consider.

1. WHO THE INVITATION IS TO
This is not an invitation for the sorted and strong but for
the weak and weary.

The passage is not explicit about what the source of this
soul weariness is. Could it be sin? Suffering? Temptation?
Perhaps just the trials of life? Given the context of where
this appears in Matthew's Gospel, there is a strong case
for it being primarily aimed at those wearied by the demands of self-righteous religion. You know, those insane

individuals who think that they can serve God in their own strength and out of their own resources (cough!), who don't really think they need verses like this one (cough, cough!).

The great news, however, is that if you're exhausted—you qualify. This invitation is directed at shattered saints like us. Praise God!

2. WHO THE INVITATION IS FROM

These words are especially sweet because of who spoke them—this invitation comes straight from the gentle, humble heart of Jesus Christ.

He is, after all, the flesh-and-blood embodiment of the God who neither breaks bruised reeds nor snuffs out faintly flickering candles (Isaiah 42:3).

He is the good shepherd who diligently searches for his lost sheep and, upon finding it, scoops it up and carries it all the way home with a joyful song on his lips (Luke 15:5).

He is the friend of sinners—irresistible to the miserable, magnetic to the pathetic and a refuge to the wretched, the distressed and the oppressed.

How amazing it is to think that the Son of God—the second Person of the Trinity, the Creator and sustainer of the universe, the glorious Saviour of the world—does not look at us in our crumpled mess and write us off. He doesn't push us away or chide us for not being strong, stable or holy enough. Instead, he draws us to himself. The passion in his heart for the lost, the lowest and least burns ever hotter and brighter. If we could fully grasp the true depths of Christ's love for us, we would not be able to stop ourselves from coming to him and clinging to him with desperate faith for all that he is worth.

3. WHAT IS BEING OFFERED

The offer that Jesus puts on the table is what our hearts most desperately need: *rest*. Rest from striving to be good enough (or pretending that we are). Rest from religion and performance-based faith. Rest from trying to earn God's favour or to pacify his anger. Rest for our weary souls. Rest in what Jesus has done for us on our behalf, through his death and resurrection. This is the gospel— the "good news".

But it gets even better: Jesus offers his commitment to serving us as a gospel coach. That's the idea behind the word "yoke"—an image of two oxen pulling together. He'll help us to live out our faith in new ways that are neither heavy nor burdensome (the absolute opposite to whatever got us into this mess in the first place!). And ultimately, he promises perfect rest with him in the bliss of his heaven when all of this is over.

Accepting this invitation—for the first time, or the thousandth time—is the initial step on a journey to being refreshed, restored and renewed by Jesus. So to all my fellow strugglers and stragglers, limping sheep and crumpled heaps—let's do this. Let's respond to the voice of the Master and take him up on his generous offer. Let's come to him, crawling if we have to, collapse at his feet and rest in his gracious embrace. Let's wrap our feeble fingers around the treasure of his beautiful gospel and refuse to let go. Let's fill our lungs with the oxygen of fresh faith. And let's start moving hopeward.

You ready?

Lord Jesus, you have invited me to come, so here I am! I come with fragile faith and in desperate need of your grace. I'm a mess, Lord—but I'm happy to be your mess. Please wrap me in your loving arms and speak to me through your word. Let me hear your voice and help me to believe. Please thrill me again with your gospel. Heal me, forgive me, restore me, I pray. Flood my heart with hope and grant rest to my weary soul. I need you, Jesus, and I love you. Amen.

REFLECTION QUESTIONS

1. What are the various factors that have caused or could cause you to crumple?

2. In the list of people at Jesus' feet, who do you most relate to? Why?

3. What has struck you afresh about Jesus' invitation to "Come to me, all who labour and are heavy laden..."?

2. RECEIVE FROM JESUS
(He gives grace to the needy)

HIS WORDS WERE KIND AND TRUE:
"I KNOW WHAT YOU'VE BEEN THROUGH.
I'VE GOT ALL THE GRACE YOU NEED
AND I'M GIVING IT TO YOU."

"Let us then with confidence draw near to the throne of grace, that we may receive mercy and find grace to help in time of need." (Hebrews 4:16)

Imagine you are about to enter the reception area of Jesus' gospel rehab. You've come here at the Master's personal invitation. As you step inside, a wave of temperate air hits you with relief. The door softly closes behind you and the din of the outside world is hushed to silence. Inside, it's bright but not glaring; warm but not stuffy. More than that, it smells incredible and feels... hopeful!

As you cast your eye around the room, you are encouraged by how many others are checked-in too. You are not alone here—there are weary saints of all ages and stages of life here, in as much need of help as you are.

You even recognise a few faces—some who have worshipped with you in church or served alongside you at different points in your life. Many of them always seemed like they were coping, thriving even, as they sought to follow Jesus. And yet here they are! Perhaps (like many of us) they had been hiding their struggles behind masks and fake smiles, only for it to all come crashing down when their resources ran dry. Like you, they are in the right place to recover.

When Jesus calls the weak and weary to "come to me" for rest, he is not merely holding out a bottle of water for us to swig in-between heavy sets at the gym. Neither is he offering a quick patch-up and pep-talk in the medical tent before shoving us back out into the heat of battle. Rather, Jesus invites us to check in to his gospel rehab for rest, recovery and renewal. The length of our stay and the treatment required will depend a lot on the state that we find ourselves in and the cause of our exhaustion in the first place.

But one thing's for sure: now we have humbly responded to Jesus' invitation to "check in", the trajectory from here truly is hopeward. There is an unspoken air of expectation here, a stirring and surprising optimism that permeates the room...

Hope does that to you!

Above the reception desk is a bright, beautiful banner emblazoned with these wonderful words:

> *Since then we have a great high priest who has passed through the heavens, Jesus, the Son of God, let us hold fast our confession. For we do not have a high priest*

> *who is unable to sympathise with our weaknesses, but one who in every respect has been tempted as we are, yet without sin. Let us then with confidence draw near to the throne of grace, that we may receive mercy and find grace to help in time of need. (Hebrews 4:14-16)*

Every eye in the room seems to be fixed on that banner, because these words hold forth the hope that each person so desperately needs.

So let's take a closer look. This chapter is going to dig into these words in a bid to truly understand the staggering grace that all who check in to the gospel rehab can hope to receive.

OUR GREAT HIGH PRIEST

Let's be in no doubt: the reason that this is the right place for recovery is because of who is at the heart of everything that happens here—the Lord Jesus:

> *Since then we have a great high priest who has passed through the heavens, Jesus, the Son of God, let us hold fast our confession. For we do not have a high priest who is unable to sympathise with our weaknesses, but one who in every respect has been tempted as we are, yet without sin. (v 14-15)*

Jesus—and Jesus alone—is the sole hope that any of us have of making it back from the crumpled mess we find ourselves in, because Jesus, the Son of God, is our *great* high priest. But what exactly does that mean?

In the Old Testament, the high priest's job was to stand in the "gap" between sinful people and a holy God. Hebrews 5:1-3 tells us that the high priest offered sacrifices to atone for the peoples' sins and gently cared for sinners in their struggles. Notably, however, no high priest was perfect and so they also had to offer sacrifices for their own sins.

This is what sets Jesus apart as a great high priest—he didn't just come to make a sacrifice for our sins, he came to *be* the sacrifice for our sins, in his death on the cross. And while he fully sympathises with us in our weakness, he does so as one who never once caved into temptation or allowed his struggle to lead him astray.

This is amazing news for people like us. We have the reassurance that our help comes from someone who perfectly understands our weaknesses and temptations, yet *also* holds the keys to navigating weakness and temptation perfectly.

Jesus totally gets us. There is not a single sin, struggle, trial or temptation that you have faced, are facing, or ever will face that could cause Jesus to shrug his shoulders and say, *I'm sorry, I can't help you because I have absolutely no idea what that must be like.* No, he has faced down every temptation imaginable, and experienced *all* kinds of suffering— yet came through it all without faltering or failing.

Just pause and meditate on that for a minute. Because of the high priestly work of Jesus, we come to a God who fully understands our human experience—even the deepest, darkest depths and murkiest, most miserable moments. Whatever it was that caused you to crumple—he can relate to it. Wow!

DRAW NEAR

I used to have a dog called Boaz who was a 45kg (99lb) unit of pure mongrel muscle. He was an amazing companion who would go everywhere with me. I loved having him by my side and he loved being with me.

Except, that is, when he'd done something wrong. Whenever he'd misbehaved he would slink back with his tail between his legs and walk several metres behind me. It could take an age for him to come back to my side and usually required reassurance from me in the form of soft words and treats.

I wonder if the reason that many of us are so slow to check into gospel rehab is because we're all a bit like Boaz. Perhaps we fear that our mess (especially if it's a mess of our own making) disgusts God to the point that he must want nothing to do with us. Sure, we still want to be with him, we just feel the need to skulk along behind him with our tails tucked shamefully between our legs.

The beauty of our great high priest is that far from being repulsed by us, his heart burns for us and his desire is for us to draw close to him or, as we say in Wales, for us to cwtch in:* *"Let us then with confidence draw near..."* (4:16).

Read those words again.

Slowly.

---

* Cwtch (rhymes with "butch" with a "k" at the beginning) is the Welsh word for cuddle.

We are encouraged to draw near and to do so "with confidence". But if you're anything like I was when I lay in a crumpled heap, the thought of drawing near to a holy God with confidence, courage or boldness probably sounds insane! In the midst of shame, the grip of fear or the paralysis of failure, how in the world could we confidently come to him, let alone "cwtch in"?

Answer: because Jesus died to make that kind of intimacy possible.

- Our sin has been paid for and our shame has been covered.

- Perfect love has been unleashed to drive our fears far away.

- Jesus himself now stands right beside us to reassure us and represent us.

- We are welcomed as cherished children, loved and accepted by the Father.

Be advised, however, that confidently drawing near does not mean that we can simply strut into God's divine presence like we somehow deserve to be there through any merit of our own. No way! Rather, we must base our confidence fully on the finished work of Jesus on the cross. When he died, "the curtain of the temple was torn in two, from top to bottom" (Matthew 27:51). This was the curtain that marked off the Holy of Holies at the heart of the temple—the place of God's presence, which only the high priest could enter. But when our great high priest died, the tearing of the curtain screamed to a wretched, rebellious world that we now have access to God's holy presence through the sacrifice of Jesus. Yet the curtain was ripped from top to bottom, not from bottom to top. In other words, it was God's doing, not ours, which is why there can be no swagger in our steps. It's all his work!

If Jesus would gladly pay with his own blood to secure access for sinners like us to "draw near" to God, the only thing that could stop us is our own pride. So this is how we should come—not skulking and not strutting, but confidently striding with footsteps emboldened by faith:

> *Therefore, brothers and sisters, since we have confidence to enter the holy places by the blood of Jesus, by the new and living way that he opened for us through the curtain, that is, through his flesh, and since we have a great priest over the house of God, let us draw near with a true heart in full assurance of faith, with our hearts sprinkled clean from an evil conscience and our bodies washed with pure water.*
> *(Hebrews 10:19-22)*

GET GRACE

So what awaits those who might dare to draw near? What should we expect? Well, here we find some of the most beautiful and reassuring words that weary and sinful saints could possibly hear:

> *Let us then with confidence draw near to the throne of grace, that we may receive mercy and find grace to help in time of need. (Hebrews 4:16)*

This is the only place in Scripture that the throne of God is given this title—and *what* a title!

It is not a throne of condemnation or criticism, nor is it a throne of disapproval or dismissal.

It's not a throne of rage or rebuke.

It's a throne of *grace*—and it's the *only* hope for weary and wayward pilgrims like us.

As we draw near to this throne, we get mercy and grace at just the right time. Or put another way, we get exactly what we need, exactly when we need it.

Mercy could be defined as "not getting what we deserve". The Scriptures are clear that men and women who have rebelled against God—that is, all of us—are by nature "children of wrath" who deserve God's just punishment (Ephesians 2:3). We deserve hell. Through his death on the cross Jesus drank the cup of God's furious wrath against sin to the very last dregs. He endured a hellish death in our place so that we need not fear God's judgment. That is mercy and it is ours in abundance in Christ.

Whatever it was that has brought you to your knees...

Whatever burdens may be crushing you...

Whatever shame may be stalking you...

Whatever regrets may be robbing you of peace...

See your Great High Priest holding out a hand of mercy, not a fist of retribution:

> *There is therefore now no condemnation for those*
> *who are in Christ Jesus. (Romans 8:1)*

But there's more! If mercy is God *not* giving us what we do deserve, grace could perhaps be defined as God giving us what we absolutely do not deserve. We deserve judgment but we receive forgiveness. We deserve to be cast out but he draws us near. We deserve hell but are now citizens of heaven. We deserve nothing from his hand yet he *"graciously give[s] us all things"* (Romans 8:32).

All things? Really?

Yes! He will provide whatever we need to thrive and live for him—strength for our weakness, healing for our wounds, peace to our troubled minds, comfort in our affliction, supernatural joy for our deepest sorrows and relentless love despite our unloveliness.

All of it is thoroughly undeserved. All of it is gloriously ours in Christ. Paul describes it this way in Philippians 4:19: "And my God will supply every need of yours according to his riches in glory in Christ Jesus."

Perhaps you had understood that you have been saved by grace (Ephesians 2:8-9). But did you know that God's grace is also the only way that weak, creaking, crumpled Christians like us are ever going to make it to the finish line? Jesus put it this way:

> *My grace is sufficient for you, for my power is made*
> *perfect in weakness. (2 Corinthians 12:9)*

The weakness that we want to escape from is the very thing that God uses to perfectly display his power, as he graciously sustains us through it.

As we draw this chapter to a close, I encourage you to come into this throne room and to gaze around in wonder. Meditate on the finished work of your great high priest, Jesus, and let his irresistible grace blow your mind and warm your heart. I don't know your story and I don't know what's brought you to this place, but I do know that this is where you need to be! I am 100% convinced that here, bowing before this throne, is the best possible place for you to be. Because Jesus is here and he has opened up the stores to all the mercy and grace you will ever need!

So why not stretch out your hand and receive it now, as you pray.

Lord Jesus, thank you for being a great high priest who knows me completely, sees my every flaw and failure, and yet draws near to me, rather than turning from me. You are so good and so kind. I know that I deserve nothing from you but I believe that your throne is a throne of grace. I bow before you with an open hand and humble, hopeful heart. Please lavish your abundant grace and mercy upon me. Restore my weary soul and give me strength to live for you. I pray these things for your glory. Amen.

REFLECTION QUESTIONS

1. Are you ready to humble yourself and "check in" to the gospel rehab? Is there anything holding you back?

2. How do you feel about Jesus being a high priest who is able to sympathise with all your weaknesses? What most struck you from this chapter?

3. What is the grace that you are desperately in need of right now?

3. ABIDE IN JESUS
(He enables us to rest)

SUCH MERCY IN HIS FACE
AS HE LAVISHED ME WITH GRACE
MY WEARY SOUL FOUND REST
IN THE WARMTH OF HIS EMBRACE.

"Abide in me..." (Jesus in John 15:4)

We've collapsed at Jesus' feet. We've checked in to the gospel rehab and are now tentatively believing that the Lord Jesus is ready and willing to dispense whatever grace we might need in order to recover and start rebuilding.

Where do we go from here? Deep down, we want nothing more than to get back on our feet, fight the good fight, run the race and start serving our Saviour with passion again... but just the thought of that probably feels exhausting right now. So what's the next step?

Answer: we need to... abide.

Let's head out of the clinic and into the garden. As you read these words from Jesus, try and count how many times the word "abide" is used. (Fair warning: you won't have enough fingers!)

I am the true vine, and my Father is the vine dresser. Every branch in me that does not bear fruit he takes away, and every branch that does bear fruit he prunes, that it may bear more fruit. Already you are clean because of the word that I have spoken to you. Abide in me, and I in you. As the branch cannot bear fruit by itself, unless it abides in the vine, neither can you, unless you abide in me. I am the vine; you are the branches. Whoever abides in me and I in him, he it is that bears much fruit, for apart from me you can do nothing. If anyone does not abide in me he is thrown away like a branch and withers; and the branches are gathered, thrown into the fire, and burned. If you abide in me, and my words abide in you, ask whatever you wish, and it will be done for you. By this my Father is glorified, that you bear much fruit and so prove to be my disciples. As the Father has loved me, so have I loved you. Abide in my love. If you keep my commandments, you will abide in my love, just as I have kept my Father's commandments and abide in his love. These things I have spoken to you, that my joy may be in you, and that your joy may be full.

This is my commandment, that you love one another as I have loved you. Greater love has no one than this, that someone lay down his life for his friends. You are my friends if you do what I command you. No longer do I call you servants, for the servant does not know what his master is doing; but I have called you friends, for all that I have heard from my Father I have made known to you. You did not choose me, but I chose you

and appointed you that you should go and bear fruit
and that your fruit should abide, so that whatever you
ask the Father in my name, he may give it to you. These
things I command you, so that you will love one
another. (John 15:1-17)

These are incredible words that, if taken to heart and applied, will change the trajectory of your whole life. That's a bold claim, but I believe it's true. So does Jesus!

1. RECOVER YOUR IDENTITY

The word "abide" appears eleven times in this passage, but what does it mean? Other Bible translations use similar words such as "remain", "stay" or "continue". Putting all of these together helps us to understand what Jesus is exhorting us to do.

This next step on the trajectory of hope is...

To rest.

To remain.

To dwell.

To abide with Jesus.

Jesus is not offering us a quick adrenaline shot in the arm before booting us back out of the door to "do better next time". No, his invitation to the weary is to come to him and to stay with him.

He's in this for the long haul.

Are we?

Let's zoom in on a few verses:

> *Abide in me, and I in you. As the branch cannot bear*
> *fruit by itself, unless it abides in the vine, neither can*
> *you, unless you abide in me. I am the vine; you are the*
> *branches. Whoever abides in me and I in him, he it is*
> *that bears much fruit, for apart from me you can do*
> *nothing. (v 4-5)*

These must be among the most humbling words in the whole Bible. I'm not the most green-fingered person, but even I know that the branch needs the vine a lot more than the vine needs the branch! Cut the branch off and it dies. The vine will survive.

And guess which we are in God's great vineyard—vine or branches?

That's right, we're the branches, and Jesus is the vine.

He's the source of all that is good and pleasant and life-giving and, as Jesus says, "Apart from me you can do nothing" (v 5). Some of us need to stick that verse on the bathroom mirror so that as we brush our teeth each morning we are reminded, through bleary eyes, of our utter reliance on Jesus.

- We bring *nothing* to the table.

- We will achieve *nothing* of significance without him.

- We can do *nothing* in and of ourselves to get back up on our feet, let alone start running again.

We live in a culture which idolises self-sufficiency and

seeks to sell us a million different ways to help ourselves. But here at the feet of Jesus we get a very different message: we are weak, finite and limited, whereas he is mighty, infinite and limitless. He is the vine; we are merely the branches.

This is humbling truth, but there is *such* rest for our souls when we accept this. We can't move the needle on God's work in the world by trying harder, doing more, or being better. The mission of Jesus does not depend on us; it depends on him. And he will not fail to do all that he has planned.

2. REDISCOVER YOUR PURPOSE

In the middle of writing this chapter, I took a break and headed down to the chapel where my wife and I lead a Bible study for new believers. One of the ladies in the group had just returned from Albania and wanted to show us a photograph of an orange tree in her father's garden.

The tree had been growing bitter oranges that were inedible, so her father had spliced in a branch from a stronger tree that was producing sweet oranges. As a result, the tree now only grows sweet oranges. Incredible! I guess her father really wanted that tree to be fruitful (and I guess God knew that I really needed an illustration for this section!).

Having seen that we are utterly dependent on Jesus, we might conclude that there's no part for us to play. Yet in this passage, Jesus talks almost as much about bearing fruit as he does about abiding. Fruitfulness, it would seem, is also really important to God:

By this my Father is glorified, that you bear much fruit and so prove to be my disciples. (v 8)

Fruitfulness matters because it glorifies God. It also matters because it proves that we are truly disciples of Jesus. The logical question then becomes: What is fruitfulness? What fruit does God want to produce in and through our lives?

It would take another book to fully answer that question, but for the purpose of this chapter let me summarise what I believe the answer is.

Love.

If you keep my commandments, you will abide in my love ... This is my commandment, that you love one another as I have loved you. Greater love has no one than this, that someone lay down his life for his friends ... These things I command you, so that you will love one another. (v 10, 12-13, 17)

A fruitful Christian life is one that is marked by an enduring, sacrificial, Christ-like love for others. And this passage is far from the only place that Jesus taught this.

*A new commandment I give to you, that you **love one another:** just as I have loved you, you also are to love one another. By this all people will know that you are my disciples, if you have love for one another.*
(John 13:34-35, my emphasis)

*You shall love the Lord your God with all your heart
and with all your soul and with all your mind. This
is the great and first commandment. And a second is
like it: **You shall love your neighbour as yourself.**
On these two commandments depend all the Law and
the Prophets. (Matthew 22:37-40, my emphasis)*

*You have heard that it was said, "You shall love your
neighbour and hate your enemy." But I say to you,
Love your enemies and pray for those who persecute
you, so that you may be sons of your Father who is in
heaven. (Matthew 5:43-45, my emphasis)*

Our purpose as Christians is to love our brothers and sisters in Christ, to love the lost and the broken all around us, and even to love our enemies. That sounds costly and exhausting—impossible, even—doesn't it?!

And it is... *if*, that is, we go about it in the wrong way. I wonder if the reason some of us are so weary is because we are desperately trying to produce the fruit of love in our own strength. We are trying to love our spouses, care for our families, serve our churches, support our colleagues and reach our communities, digging deep into our own puny reserves, all the while failing to grasp the humble, simple truth that the key to fruitfulness is not striving, but abiding.

Let me say it again: the primary message of this passage is not that we should bear fruit but that we should abide. Fruitfulness is merely a by-product of abiding. Jesus tells us again and again to abide in him but then, more specifically, to *"abide in my love"* (John 15:10). He grows the fruit of love *in* us as we soak up his love *for* us.

What does abiding in the love of Jesus look like? It means reading and listening and speaking and singing and dancing and delighting in the light of his love. It means refusing to allow our hearts to be enticed away by lesser loves. It means leaning ever more deeply into Jesus' love and unashamedly revelling in it with neither fear nor restraint.

It's only as we rest in his unfailing, unconditional love for us that we will have the capacity to enduringly love others. John later put it this way:

We love because he first loved us. (1 John 4:19)

Isn't that just so liberating? We were never called to be superheroes! We are simply branches grafted by faith into the vine of Christ, the true hero. We are called to abide in him—to draw on his infinite strength and limitless resources—in order that he might produce the fruit of love in our lives, for the glory of God and the good of others.

3. REFRAME YOUR PAIN

One of the joys of my life has been coaching a junior football team for my youngest son and his friends. The Covid lockdown of 2020 was tough for the boys because they lost a lot of the social benefits of being part of a team. But one of the other things they lost was match fitness. So when lockdown lifted and we were finally able to start training again, we spent several weeks just focusing on fitness drills.

They hated it and, to be honest, I didn't really enjoy making them work so hard either. But I knew that if they didn't get their fitness levels back up, they were not going to be able to perform to the best of their abilities on match day. I can't remember how many times I set them off to run another lap of the pitch with these words ringing in their ears:

"You hate me now, but you'll thank me for it later!"

Keep those words in mind as we meet one final character in this passage:

> *I am the true vine, and my Father is the vine dresser.*
> *Every branch in me that does not bear fruit he takes*
> *away, and every branch that does bear fruit he prunes,*
> *that it may bear more fruit. (v 1-2)*

Jesus introduces his Father to us as the "vine dresser" or gardener—the one who is ultimately responsible for cultivating the vine so that it bears maximum fruit. We are told just two things about the work of the vine dresser.

First, he cuts away fruitless branches that have withered because they no longer abide in the vine. These branches are burned in fire (v 6). These represent those people who were never truly in Christ. Their fate is both tragic and sobering.

But it is the second action of the vine dresser that I want us to focus on: he prunes fruitful branches that do abide, in order to make them more fruitful. Pruning involves cutting away dead or unhealthy pieces of the branch. It is painful for the vine but essential if fruitfulness is to be maximised.

In the same way, God is committed to cutting away what is dead and unhealthy in our lives in order to make us more fruitful. It is short-term pain for long-term gain, and if we can see it from that perspective, it will help us to reframe the pain, suffering and brokenness that afflicts us here and now.

What burdens have been crushing you?

What wounds have never really healed?

What was it that brought you crashing down, or threatens to?

The shame of sin—committed by you or against you? The impact of unexpected tragedy or the onslaught of circumstances outside of your control? Is it physical pain? Personal weakness? A broken heart? The weight of unrealistic expectations? Or is it simply the gradual, grinding slump into exhaustion as you try... and repeatedly fail... to hold it all together? Chances are it's a perfect storm of much of the above.

Whatever is wearing you down, I want you to see the beauty in what Jesus is saying here. Your pain is not pointless—it is serving a divine purpose. There is a loving vine dresser who is at work behind the scenes to make you more fruitful than you could ever dream. He can be trusted. Knowing this might not take the pain away, but it can certainly help us to reframe it: to see it as productive rather than destructive; surgical rather than indiscriminate. It might be hard to believe in the moment, but none of your pain is wasted. When you know the heart of the vine dresser, you grow to trust the work of his hands.

Many people throughout the Scriptures learned to view their pain in this way—although often only in hindsight:

> *As for you, you meant evil against me, but God meant it for good, to bring it about that many people should be kept alive, as they are today. (Joseph in Genesis 50:20)*

> *It is good for me that I was afflicted,*
> *that I might learn your statutes.*
> *(The psalmist in Psalm 119:71)*

> *For the moment all discipline seems painful rather than pleasant, but later it yields the peaceful fruit of righteousness to those who have been trained by it.*
> *(The writer to the Hebrews in Hebrews 12:11)*

There are many more similar examples of men and women in the Bible who, by faith, were able to reframe their pain and trace the hand of a loving God through their struggles and sorrows. I know that this truth does not remove your brokenness, but it can redeem it. My prayer is that it will.

4. REJOICE!

While we may not see the fruit of God's pruning right now, we don't need to wait in hopeless despair. In the middle of this amazing passage, Jesus encourages us with these words:

These things I have spoken to you, that my joy may be in you, and that your joy may be full. (John 15:11)

As we abide in Jesus—as we rest and revel in his unbreakable love for us—we can experience his joy even during the pain of pruning.

In another part of the Bible, James wrote this to a group of struggling believers:

Count it all joy, my brothers, when you meet trials of various kinds, for you know that the testing of your faith produces steadfastness. And let steadfastness have its full effect, that you may be perfect and complete, lacking in nothing. (James 1:2-4)

The thought of joy may seem impossible right now. But Jesus and James both want to encourage you that God is doing something promising in your life! You may feel stuck, helpless and exhausted—but if there is pruning taking place you can rest assured that God is committed to increasing your fruitfulness. He wants you to grow! The pruning is painful, but with each loving "snip" the vine dresser is reminding you that he is tenderly at work in your life, making known his deep love to you and fulfilling his perfect plans for you.

And so we rejoice. We rejoice in the relief that we could never do any of it on our own anyway—and we don't have to. We rejoice that God is invested and involved in our lives, pruning and watering and caring for us. We rejoice that he calls us his friends, not his servants (John 15:15).

We rejoice that we can ask for anything in his name, and he gives it to us (v 16). We rejoice that he chose us (v 16). There is still much joy to be found!

Be encouraged, dear friend, that Jesus does not just invite you to come, he wants you to stay: to abide in him and to bury yourself in his love. As you do so, may you lose your misplaced sense of self-importance and see yourself as you truly are—yes, a trophy of his amazing grace, but a branch, not the vine. It's ok to be weak. It's ok to be a mess. It's ok to not have all the answers.

It's ok...

Abide securely in the vine.

Rest in his love.

And joy will follow.

Trust the hand of the vine dresser—he's not finished with you yet!

Lord Jesus, I confess that my soul can be so restless at times. Thank you that your desire is to abide with me and for me to abide in you and to rest in your love. Please help me to embrace this privilege and keep my heart from straying after lesser loves. Help me to trust the Father's work as he cuts away those things in my life that stunt my growth. I long for my life to be increasingly marked by the fruit of your love, so that others may taste and see that you are good. I gladly choose to abide in you. Amen.

REFLECTION QUESTIONS

1. What comes more naturally to you—abiding or striving?

2. What is your response to the notion that apart from Jesus you can do nothing?

3. How have you seen God "pruning" you recently? Does the thought of a vine dresser being at work in your life help you to see your pain in a more hopeful light?

4. FEAST ON JESUS
(He feeds the hungry)

*"Whoever feeds on my flesh and drinks my blood
has eternal life." (Jesus in John 6:54)*

I try to get to the gym on a regular basis, although these days it's not so much about getting hench as simply trying to stave off premature death!

I have a love-hate relationship with my gym. I love training and feel great when I've pushed hard and made gains, but I hate everything leading up to training. And I really hate it when progress seems to be going backwards.

I had a session recently where I could barely lift weights I had "crushed" only a few weeks earlier. I was so annoyed. Then Dave, the gym owner, strolled past me and it all made sense.

As is often the case, Dave had a small tub of food in his hand. Unlike me—who only eats a few times a day—Dave tends to eat small portions of good food (usually chicken and rice) regularly throughout the day. This means that his body is always ready to work because it's constantly fully loaded with carbohydrates and protein—essential for exerting energy and developing strength.

I, on the other hand, had only just managed to eat a small piece of jam on toast earlier in what was a very busy day. Consequently, I was running on fumes and my body was unable to do what I was demanding of it.

I share this because this next phase of the hopeward trajectory is where we seek to regain our strength and get back on our feet again. So it's crucial that we do everything possible to stack our system with the right kind of fuel. Spiritually speaking, we need a lot more than jam on toast. So what exactly should we be digging into?

Well, as every Sunday-school kid will tell you, the answer is always Jesus.

Or to be more specific...

> The person of Jesus.

> The work of Jesus.

> The words of Jesus.

We find each of these key ingredients in the sixth chapter of John's Gospel. This epic chapter starts with Jesus feeding 5,000+ people with a little boy's packed lunch—a miracle that is almost as famous as it is phenomenal. Then in verses 16-21 Jesus literally takes a stroll across the tempestuous Sea of Tiberias, much to the terror of his disciples. (Side note: these are two of the first videos I'm going to ask Jesus if we can rewatch in heaven!)

The next day, while still picking fish out from between their teeth, the same crowd come looking for Jesus again. They finally catch up with him at the synagogue in Capernaum and the rest of the chapter records this encounter.

Let's dive in...

1. THE PERSON OF JESUS

Knowing that the crowd were merely looking for more miraculous munch, Jesus calls them out on it: "Truly, truly, I say to you, you are seeking me, not because you saw signs, but because you ate your fill of the loaves" (v 26). In other words, *You only want me for my miracles!*

As the conversation continues, the crowd demand that Jesus dish up some heavenly bread in the same way that Moses had done in the wilderness (see Exodus 16). Here's what Jesus has to say to that:

I am the bread of life; whoever comes to me shall not hunger, and whoever believes in me shall never thirst ... Your fathers ate the manna in the wilderness, and they died. This is the bread that comes down from heaven, so that one may eat of it and not die. I am the living bread that came down from heaven. If anyone eats of this bread, he will live for ever. And the bread that I will give for the life of the world is my flesh.
(John 6:35; 49-51)

Jesus is saying that he didn't just come to give bread but to be bread. He is not merely the source of the food, he is the actual substance of it. He is not just the giver, he is the gift itself. And what a gift—bread from heaven that makes us live for ever! Only Jesus can satisfy our spiritual hunger and replenish our thirsty souls. Only he can fulfil our deepest desires and supply the strength we need to endure.

Jesus is enough.

He really is.

I wonder if some of us have ended up exhausted, frustrated and defeated because we have been stuffing our lives with the spiritual junk food of this world rather than seeking after Jesus. Maybe we've numbed our minds through doom-scrolling on our phones. Or worn ourselves out in the pursuit of wealth, comfort or acclaim. Or perhaps our vain attempts at self-improvement have failed to deliver the results we had hoped for.

I wonder if this is what the 19-century hymnwriter Emma Bevan was getting at when she penned these lyrics:

> *I tried the broken cisterns, Lord,*
> *But, ah, the waters failed;*
> *Even as I stooped to drink they fled,*
> *And mocked me as I wailed.*
>
> *Now none but Christ can satisfy,*
> *None other name for me!*
> *There's love, and life, and lasting joy,*
> *Lord Jesus, found in Thee.*

Let's pause here and ask ourselves some questions. Might we be more like the crowd than we care to admit?

- What do we really want from Jesus?

- Do we want him or do we only want what he can give us?

- Are we looking for a temporary fix or eternal fulfilment?

- Is Jesus really enough for us? How can we be sure?

And if you don't know the answer to those, maybe these will help:

- When you feel unloved or unloveable, is it enough to know that Jesus still loves you?

- When it feels like something is missing, is Jesus' presence with you still precious?

- When life is wretched, is the name of Jesus still beautiful to you?

Your answers to these questions are critical. If you just want Jesus to be some kind of glorified vending machine to bless you with your own "little miracle", helping you to get your life back on track before happily carrying on without him, you are destined for disappointment. Jesus doesn't play that game and it will only be a matter of time before you crumple again.

If however, your heart chimes with Peter—who basically says to Jesus, *You're all we've got and you're all we need!* (v 68-69)—then get ready to sink your teeth into the meal your soul has been craving and prepare to grow in strength, stature and faith.

2. THE WORK OF JESUS

As the conversation in John 6 continues, Jesus' statement "the bread that I will give for the life of the world is my flesh" (v 51) really livens things up. The crowd gets agitated: "How can this man give us his flesh to eat?" (v 52). I mean, it's a legitimate question. We need to consider Jesus' answer, but strap in because things are about to get weird...

Truly, truly, I say to you, unless you eat the flesh of the Son of Man and drink his blood, you have no life in you. Whoever feeds on my flesh and drinks my blood has eternal life, and I will raise him up on the last day. For my flesh is true food, and my blood is true drink. Whoever feeds on my flesh and drinks my blood abides in me, and I in him. As the living Father sent me, and I live because of the Father, so whoever feeds on me, he also will live because of me. This is the bread that came down from heaven, not like the bread the fathers ate, and died. Whoever feeds on this bread will live for ever. (v 53-58)

Yeah, you read that right: Jesus just said that we need to eat his flesh and drink his blood!

What does that even mean?!

Don't worry, Jesus is not endorsing cannibalism. What he is doing, however, is helping us to fully understand what it means to consume the food that is essential for our growth.

Those of us who have been around church for a while will know that the concept of eating Jesus' body and drinking his blood is commonly connected to the Lord's Supper or "Communion".

The Lord's Supper is significant because of what it reminds us of—the life of Jesus given on the cross to rescue sinners (us) from the power of sin and death. The bread symbolises his body that was broken, ripped, torn and pierced for us. The blood represents his precious, innocent blood, poured out for the forgiveness of all our sins. It's a meal that should invoke both deep gratitude and epic joy. This was the great saving work that Jesus came to do; the purpose for which he came into the world.

Without the cross there would be no forgiveness for the filthy. No redemption for rebels. No grace for God's enemies. No hope of heaven. No healing for the broken-hearted. No mercy for the messed-up. And no second-chance saloon for sinners.

The cross is such good news for crumpled heaps like us because it is here, at the foot of the cross, that we can finally be free of our burdens.

We can move on from the agony and shame that accompanies so much of our brokenness as we come to the one who was broken for us.

We can look our fear in the eye and repel it by the

power of the perfect love of Jesus displayed at the cross (Romans 5:8).

We can get shot of our sin—all of it—because Jesus' blood has paid for the lot.

We can own our weaknesses—all of them—knowing that they actually qualify us to receive God's mercy because "while we were still *weak*, at the right time Christ died for the ungodly" (Romans 5:6, emphasis mine).

We can cease striving to earn God's smile through frenzied religious activity because Christ has robed us in his perfect righteousness and the Father now beams over us with the same degree of delight that he reserves for his beloved Son.

Jesus' instruction to eat his body and drink his blood is an invitation to feast on his goodness. To gorge ourselves on his grace. To revel in his love, and stuff ourselves with the life-giving, soul-satisfying, wondrous work of his cross.

The table is open to all who are humble enough to come empty-handed to take what is offered "without money and without price" (Isaiah 55:1). It's open to all who are brave enough to acknowledge their weakness and confess their need of a Saviour; to all who would happily sing along with Emma Bevan, "Now none but Christ can satisfy, None other name for me!"

Hungry?

The table is laid.

Come to the cross and tuck in!

3. THE WORDS OF JESUS

Back to the story in John 6. Sadly, not everyone was down with what Jesus had to say. First, they grumbled (v 41), then disputed (v 52), then decried his "hard" teaching (v 60), until eventually many of them "turned back and no longer walked with him" (v 66). We see the same thing happen in our present day. If we're honest, there may even be traces of these attitudes in our own hearts when it comes to some of the tougher teachings of the Bible.

As Jesus watches many of his "disciples" disappear in a cloud of dust and disgruntlement, he turns to the twelve who remain and gives them the option to stick or twist: "Do you want to go away as well?" (v 67). Responding on behalf of the others, Peter replies: "Lord, to whom shall we go? You have the words of eternal life, and we have believed, and have come to know, that you are the Holy One of God" (v 68-69).

I am currently writing this chapter in the best coffee shop in Cardiff. It's run by two friends of mine who bought a brothel and converted it into a coffee and wine bar. As baristas they really know what they're doing, but trust me—you might come here for the coffee but you'll stay for the cookies! They are baked fresh every day with ingredients that complement the flavour notes of whatever the current house espresso may be. New coffee shops pop up all the time in Cardiff, but I won't be taking my custom anywhere else—because when you've tasted the best, why go elsewhere?

This is kind of what Peter was saying. *We've consumed your teaching, tasted your truth and gobbled up your grace.*

There's nothing else we'd rather eat and no one else we'd rather be with.

Is that how we feel about the words of Jesus?

By "the words of Jesus" I don't just mean the specific teachings that came out of Jesus' mouth—the so-called "red letters". Rather, I mean the entirety of the Scriptures, which all point to him.

No one understood this better than the two disciples who enjoyed a roving Bible study with the resurrected Jesus on the road to Emmaus, during which, "beginning with Moses and all the Prophets, he interpreted to them in all the Scriptures the things concerning himself" (Luke 24:27).

Similarly, Paul also raved about the value of the Bible in its entirety: "All Scripture is God-breathed and is useful for teaching, rebuking, correcting and training in righteousness, so that the servant of God may be thoroughly equipped for every good work" (2 Timothy 3:16-17, NIV).

We need the Bible—all of it—if we are going to grow in grace and keep heading hopeward.

Peter knew it. Those two disciples knew it. Paul knew it.

But do you know it?

If you've been a Christian for a while, it's easy for the Bible to begin to feel a little flat. If that's you, perhaps you need to pray for God to whet your appetite for his word once again. Plead with him to cause you to crave it like a starving man craves bread. Below is a selection of verses that I hope helps to underscore the beautiful truth that God's word provides essential nourishment for weak and weary souls as they seek to press on hopeward.

WHEN YOU ARE TEMPTED

How can a young person stay on the path of purity?
*   By living according to your word. (Psalm 119:9, NIV)*

WHEN YOU FEEL DOWN AND OUT

My soul clings to the dust;
*   give me life according to your word! (v 25)*

IF SORROW HAS EXHAUSTED YOU

My soul melts away for sorrow;
*   strengthen me according to your word! (v 28)*

WHEN YOU ARE BEING TAUNTED AND HUMILIATED

Let your steadfast love come to me, O LORD,
*   your salvation according to your promise;*
then shall I have an answer for him who taunts me,
*   for I trust in your word. (v 41-42)*

WHEN ALL SEEMS LOST

My soul longs for your salvation;
*   I hope in your word. (v 81)*

WHEN ANXIOUS ABOUT THE PRESENT OR THE FUTURE

Your word is a lamp to my feet
  and a light to my path. (v 105)

WHEN YOU ARE BEATEN DOWN AND AFFLICTED

I am severely afflicted;
  give me life, O LORD, according to your word!
                                        (v 107)

WHEN YOU FEEL FEARFUL AND VULNERABLE

You are my hiding place and my shield;
  I hope in your word. (v 114)

IF YOU ARE CONFLICTED AND CONFUSED

Let my cry come before you, O LORD;
  give me understanding according to your word!
                                        (v 169)

It is staggering that all those verses are found in just one chapter of the Bible—Psalm 119—and all of them illustrate just how crucial Scripture is to strengthen and sustain us.

So the Bible is important—but how do we actually go about feeding on it? This same psalm offers some really helpful verses that teach us how to find and feast on the food of God's word.

1. SEEK

> *I rejoice at your word*
> *like one who finds great spoil. (v 162)*

We need to trawl for truth like treasure. I don't mean sub-scribing to snappy podcasts or attending inspiring confer-ences (as helpful as those things can be). I mean rolling up our sleeves and digging daily into God's word on the hunt for gospel goodness to consume. But we don't only do this alone: let's be praying for those who are cooking up the sermons and Bible studies in our churches each week and then let's rock up with hungry hearts ready to be filled.

2. STORE

> *I have stored up your word in my heart,*
> *that I might not sin against you. (v 11)*

Feasting on God's word isn't a once-a-day or once-a-week activity that we finish up and move on from. We're meant to "store up" God's word in our hearts so that it shapes how we live.

Is your heart a refrigerator that's stocked with gospel fuel because, like Dave the gym owner, you're always raiding it to make sure you have good food to hand? Do you de-light in, chew on and put to work the word of God in your life? Or has some of that food been on the shelf at the back of the fridge for too long? What practical steps could you take to bring what you hear and what you read into the rest of your day?

3. SING

My tongue will sing of your word,
for all your commandments are right. (v 172)

Part of our spiritual workout should be worship. Or to use a different image, feasting on God's word should be a spiritual festival experience—the promises of Scripture are meant to get you amped! As you read the Bible, look for truths about God that make you want to praise him. Then open your mouth and do it! Pray about it; sing about it; tell someone else about it—and feel your joy increase as you do. Why not start right now with one of these verses from Psalm 119?

KEEP MOVING

Dear friend, I know that you are worn out and weary. I know this journey we're on together might feel daunting, scary even. I know that coming to Jesus, flopping at his feet and staying there is tempting. But just like we can't stay under the duvet on a wintry work-day morning, neither can we stay here. We need to keep moving hopeward.

We've come to Jesus.

We've humbly sought his grace.

We've chosen abiding over striving.

We have feasted on the Bread of Life.

Now it's time to take the next step.

Ready? Ok, let's go...

Lord Jesus, I am weak and spiritually impoverished. I have tasted too much of the junk food of this world and it has left me sickly and dissatisfied. Please forgive me. I turn to you now with a renewed hunger for you and fresh appetite for your gospel. I ask that you would fill me and thrill me once again. Strengthen my faith, replenish my energy and restore my love for you, I pray. May your strength be perfected in my weakness so that you might rightly receive all the glory for anything good that comes from my life. Amen.

REFLECTION QUESTIONS

1. What kinds of junk food might you have been snacking on that have left you spiritually weak and malnourished?

2. Does the gospel of Jesus still taste good to you? If so, what do you love about it? If not, why not?

3. How easy do you find it to get into the Bible? Who/what could help you to dig deeper?

5. GROW IN JESUS

(Be strengthened by his Spirit, with his people, in his love)

EMBOLDENED BY THE SAINTS
EMPOWERED BY THE SPIRIT
I BEGAN TO GRASP THE LOVE OF CHRIST —
A LOVE THAT KNOWS NO LIMITS.

"To know the love of Christ that surpasses knowledge..." (Ephesians 3:19)

Several years ago, I was coerced into doing Tough Mudder—an eleven-mile assault course that exhausts you, freezes you, electrocutes you and generally makes you miserable! My arthritis-riddled ankles made me question the wisdom of my involvement, but I agreed to do it anyway to raise money for charity. I purchased a pair of military-grade marching boots to shore up my glass ankles and commenced my training.

The day came. I won't bore you with the details of my mediocre exploits, but I did manage to complete the course. Just. However, I would *not* have crossed the finish line if I had been running alone.

I ran with three friends—all of whom were younger and fitter than me. The camaraderie I enjoyed with these brothers was invaluable as we navigated the course together. We encouraged one another through literal blood, sweat and tears and the guys all graciously slowed their pace to keep me with them.

However, about ten miles deep into the race, there was one obstacle that was simply beyond me. We had to scale a giant quarter pipe (think skatepark) that was soaked in water and more than double head height.

By this stage I had been running on empty for several miles and my sodden combat boots felt like concrete blocks lashed to my feet. I told the guys I would give it one go and that if I didn't make it they should finish the race without me. With a mixture of pride and ugly jealousy I watched as each of them ran up the ramp and scrambled over the top like carefree kids playing soldiers behind the sofa.

Then it was my turn.

My teammates were all at the top of the ramp screaming at me to give it my best shot.

I drew several deep breaths and charged...

It was more of a shuffle than a sprint (think walrus), but with everything I had left I lunged at the ramp or, more specifically, at my friends who were hanging over the rail at the top with outstretched hands. Miraculously, my mate Jim, a former Royal Marine, managed to clasp my hand and dangle me dead-weight as the other lads grabbed whatever limbs and clothing they could. Then together, with inglorious grunts and groans, they man-handled me over the top. It was both pathetic and magnificent all at the same time.

I made it across the Tough Mudder finish line—but *only* because of my friends.

Why share that story? Well, as the title of this chapter indicates, this next stage of our hopeward trajectory is *growth*. We have come to Jesus and are now receiving from him, resting in him and feasting on him. We now need to grow stronger before we start walking—and then running—again. But growth is not something we can achieve alone. We need help. That's what the apostle Paul is going to teach us:

> *For this reason I bow my knees before the Father, from whom every family in heaven and on earth is named, that according to the riches of his glory he may grant you to be strengthened with power through his Spirit in your inner being, so that Christ may dwell in your hearts through faith—that you, being rooted and grounded in love, may have strength to comprehend with all the saints what is the breadth and length and height and depth, and to know the love of Christ that surpasses knowledge, that you may be filled with all the fullness of God. (Ephesians 3:14-19)*

Paul wrote these words to the church in the city of Ephesus. Paul spent around three years teaching in Ephesus (Acts 19 – 20), during which time he saw repentance, baptisms, wild miracles and demonic beatdowns. All this culminated in a riot that led to him leaving the city, never to return. This letter, however, reveals that the Ephesian church remained close to his heart. The snippet above shows him praying fervently for them to grow ever deeper in their knowledge of the love of Christ. And this kind of growth was going to require the help of friends: namely, the Spirit and the saints.

1. SPIRIT

Read the passage above again. Paul knew that the kind of growth he wanted for the Ephesians was something that only God—in all his glorious Tri-unity—could accomplish. Paul gets on his knees and pleads with the *Father* to commission the *Holy Spirit* to make the believers stronger in order that they might receive *Christ* and fully know his love for them.

None of us have the capacity in and of ourselves to receive Christ into our lives or to truly grasp the magnitude of his love. We could sooner hold the sun, moon and stars to our chests than handle the Son of the Most High God dwelling within us! Such power, glory and holy intensity would be more than any sinner could endure. No, to receive Christ we need to be supernaturally strengthened—a work that only the Holy Spirit can do.

A helpful picture to have in mind here is that of a potter. To watch a potter take a lump of clay and shape it into something beautiful is truly mesmerising, but once that clay has taken on its new form it is still not fit for purpose. In fact, if you were to pour piping hot coffee into the new creation it would quickly disintegrate. First, it needs to be strengthened by extreme heat in a kiln.

The Bible speaks about believers in a similar way. Apart from God we are mere clay, but in the hands of the great potter we become vessels that have been hand-crafted to contain the greatest treasure of all—Jesus Christ (Isaiah 64:8; 2 Corinthians 4:7). But to bear such precious treasure requires the strengthening grace of God the Holy Spirit in our lives.

If Christ is dwelling in your heart through faith, it is *only* because the Father has graciously sent the Spirit to enable it. It is *he* who has prepared you to host the Creator of the cosmos in your being and who empowers you to continue to do so. It is he who will root you and ground you, so that you can know more and more of his awe-inspiring love.

Wow!

2. SAINTS

However, such love cannot be grasped alone. If we are to grow stronger in the love of Christ, we need all the help we can get, and God, in his wise kindness, has not only granted us his Spirit, he has also given us the saints— that is, other ordinary followers of Jesus:

> ... that you, being rooted and grounded in love, may have strength to comprehend with all the saints what is the breadth and length and height and depth, and to know the love of Christ that surpasses knowledge, that you may be filled with all the fullness of God.
> (Ephesians 3:17-19)

My family loves going to the cinema. There's just something about the big-screen experience that can't be rivalled. But equally enjoyable is the post-film review in the car on the way home. One of the kids will recall the funny bits, another will rave about the epic action sequences. My wife, Michelle, may comment on the character development. And me? Well, I usually just weep quietly and try not to think about how much the whole thing cost!

The reason that we are all impacted by different aspects of the same film is because although we are family, we are all different. Each of us brings our individual personality, perspective and life experience to the table. I see things that they don't, while they see things that I *never* would without them. A film is better understood and more fully appreciated when experienced together.

If that is true of a movie, how much more is that going to be true of the love of Christ? So many of the most compelling gospel insights that I have gleaned over the years have not come through personal study but by "tossing the ball around" with other brothers and sisters as we grappled with the Scriptures together. To grasp God's love, we need the church.

WHEN CHURCH HURTS

Before we go any further, I want to acknowledge that this is going to be a really challenging section of the book for some readers. While you might be comfortable with the prospect of you and the Holy Spirit working out how to put your life back together, the thought of involving others in the process is a different matter entirely. It may be that the behaviour of other people (even, sadly, other Christians) was a significant factor in your crumpling. Maybe the church broke you down when she should have been building you up.

If that has been your experience, please know that I write these words with your pain very much in mind. I have walked and wept with enough shattered saints (and have enough scars of my own) to know that for some of you reading this, the damage will be very real and the wounds may still be very raw. Abusive leaders, hypocritical believers, hurtful words, cold shoulders... I don't know what happened to you, but if the church has hurt you in *any* way, I am deeply sorry. I don't underestimate how that might have left you feeling about church.

There is so much more that can be said on this difficult subject than I can fit into these few paragraphs, but please be assured that I am certainly *not* encouraging you to put yourself in harm's way or to trust yourself to someone who has proved themselves to be untrustworthy in the past. Far from it.

But I would be unloving as a brother and unfaithful in my task to point you hopeward if I didn't seek to urge you not to give up on the church. Scripture is clear that the church, despite all her mess and mayhem, is still the focus of Christ's fierce passion—and he was under no illusions what kind of bride he was getting when he died for her on the cross.

If the idea of connecting with church again is scary then start small. Perhaps get together with a "safe" Christian friend and ask them to pray with you about it. And if you can start attending church again, don't feel like you need to let your guard down straight away. Trust is lost quickly and rebuilt very slowly, so be as cautious as you need to be. It may be that you need to find a different local church to be part of—but please don't abandon church completely. To turn our backs on her will ultimately stunt our growth and limit our capacity to both receive and revel in Jesus' deep, deep love for us.

THE LOVE OF CHRIST

The specific purpose that drove Paul to get on his knees and plead with the Father to strengthen us by his Spirit was so that, together "with all the saints", we might be able to fully comprehend the incomprehensible love of the Son. Stop and think about that for a moment. How is it even possible "to know" the love that "surpasses knowledge" (Ephesians 3:19)?

Paul helps us by holding up the love of Jesus and turning it like a gemstone, in order that four gorgeous facets of that jewel might take our collective breath away:

> ... that you, being rooted and grounded in love, may have strength to comprehend with all the saints what is the breadth and length and height and depth, and to know the love of Christ that surpasses knowledge, that you may be filled with all the fullness of God. (v 17-19)

Just like it takes a whole family to appreciate a good movie, it takes a church to truly grasp the staggering beauty of God's love. So let's take a peek at some of the facets of this precious stone and consider how we can grow in that love together.

FACET 1: THE BREADTH OF THE LOVE OF CHRIST

Just how broad is the love of Jesus? Perhaps the most famous verse in the Bible would be helpful to consider here:

> *For God so loved the world, that he gave his only Son, that whoever believes in him should not perish but have eternal life. (John 3:16)*

Jesus is the flesh-and-blood evidence that God loves the whole world. His love is wide enough to welcome in all manner of sinners, sufferers, stragglers and strays. There is not a single person on planet Earth so murky and messed up that their pitiful state places them beyond the reach of the love of Christ. And each week, as we gather with our church, we get to look around and marvel at how God has drawn so many different people from so many different walks of life to him.

And those weekly gatherings are just a sneak preview of an even greater gathering ahead. Heaven will be populated by people of every tribe, language, nation, skin-tone and culture the world has ever known. Saints from *every* imaginable background will be there basking in the glory of the risen, conquering Son of God—and the *only* thing that we will have in common is that *none* of us would have made it were it not for *him*, and the breathtaking breadth of *his* love for global citizens of all stripes!

How wide is the love of Christ?

Worldwide!

FACET 2: THE LENGTH OF THE LOVE OF CHRIST

To measure the length of God's love let's turn to Psalm 136. This anonymous masterpiece from Israel's hymnbook is an absolute banger. It takes the worshipper on a journey of praise, starting with the good God who existed before the creation of the universe, then going on to tremble at his power in creation, marvel at his mercy in redemption, celebrate his victory over multiple enemies, and rejoice in his gracious provision—all culminating with a vision of God enthroned in heaven, our eternal home!

What makes this psalm particularly impactful and memorable, however, is the refrain "… his steadfast love endures for ever" (v 1). It appears after every single line of every single verse—a total of 26 times! In other words, what the psalmist most wanted us to know about God's love is that, like God, it's eternal.

God's love will never run out, never end and never fail. And again, being in community helps us to see this even more clearly. As we read about believers in the Bible, learn about Christians from history, and get alongside older saints in our church who have been walking with Jesus for decades, we hear stories of how God has remained faithful from generation to generation.

How long is the love of Christ?

For ever!

FACET 3: THE HEIGHT OF THE LOVE OF CHRIST

When I was a kid, I would measure the size of things by comparing them with the largest thing my tiny mind could comprehend. Is it as tall as my dad? As big as a mountain? Higher than the moon?

When it comes to measuring the height of Christ's love, however, what scale could we possibly use? Psalm 103:11 is pretty much as good as it gets:

> *For as high as the heavens are above the earth,*
>   *so great is his steadfast love towards those who fear*
>   *him.*

The "heavens" that David refers to here are the stars, planets, galaxies, quasars, nebula and all the other mind-blowing mysteries of deep space that make up the universe. God's love for us is truly cosmic.

When I searched "How wide is the universe?" on Google, this was the first thing that came up:

> *Well, the observable universe is currently 93*
> *billion light years across. The whole universe is*
> *probably infinite. (https://www.britannica.com/*
> *video/185400/universe)*

One light year is roughly 5.88 trillion miles, so multiply that by 93 billion and you may just about have calculated your way to the edge of the observable universe—that means you will have reached the limit of what our most powerful telescopes and technology can currently handle.

So how big is the universe including all the non-observable bits? Apparently it's "probably infinite"!

Think about that for a minute...

If the universe is beyond anything our minds could ever fathom, then God's love is also beyond anything our minds could possibly fathom. If the universe is infinite, then God's love is also infinite. You will have covered every intergalactic inch, mastered every meteoric mystery and observed every other-worldly oddity in the entire cosmos before you can say that you have truly reached the summit of God's love for us in Christ.

Good luck with that!

How high is the love of Christ?

To infinity and beyond!

FACET 4: THE DEPTH OF THE LOVE OF CHRIST

The final facet of the jewel that Paul seeks to dazzle us with is the depth of the love of Christ. How do we measure that?

Perhaps a more helpful question might be: just how low was he willing to go for us?

Here is how Jesus would answer that question:

> *No one has ascended into heaven except he who descended from heaven, the Son of Man. (John 3:13)*

Jesus stepped down from the purity and security of heaven, descending into the dirty obscurity of our tragic, tainted world, to seek and to save rogues and rebels like us. The King of kings came to serve us, his sworn enemies. Then he went even lower: he died a gruesome death in our place on the cross before being laid limp and lifeless in a tomb.

God shows his love for us in that while we were still sinners, Christ died for us. (Romans 5:8)

Despite rising again and ascending back to the glory of heaven, Jesus retains the wounds of his crucifixion—an eternal reminder to all those who make it home to heaven just how *loved* we are.

How deep is the love of Christ?

Deeper than death!

GROWING TOGETHER IN CHRIST'S LOVE

Jesus' love for us is wider, longer, higher and deeper than we could ever grasp on our own. But God, in his kindness, has given us not only his Spirit but a church full of saints—believers who are different from us in so many ways, but who are loved just as deeply by Jesus. These are the people God uses to show us his love in all its many facets. And sometimes, like at Tough Mudder, these are the people God uses to haul us over obstacles or gently lift us to our feet when we're lying in a heap.

Gospel growth is a community project. Both the Spirit *and* the saints are vital if we are going to develop the strength needed for the journey ahead.

I pray that, empowered by the Spirit and alongside trusted brothers and sisters, you would start to gaze again at the jewel of the love of Christ. And that by doing so you would know the strength of God himself rising up within you, energising your weary soul, healing your broken heart, filling you with all the fullness of God and granting you supernatural, surprising faith to take the next step on your hopeward journey.

Lord Jesus, I want to grow in my love for you. But I recognise that I cannot achieve this alone—I need help. I ask that the Holy Spirit would be at work in me, to strengthen my faith so that you might dwell in me and that I might treasure you above all things. Please help me to love my brothers and sisters in Christ like you do. Please give me the grace to play my part in the life of the church, in order that we might grasp the greatness of your love for us, and continually revel in it together. Amen.

REFLECTION QUESTIONS

1. In what ways have you known the strengthening work of the Holy Spirit in your life?

2. In what ways have other believers helped you to grow in love for Christ? Thank God for them.

3. Are there any ways in which other believers hurt you and caused you to question God's love? Bring your wounds to God in prayer and ask him for supernatural healing, the grace to forgive and the strength to learn to love the church again.

4. Which facet of Christ's love are you most dazzled by right now, and why?

6. WALK WITH JESUS
(He is with us and for us)

"FOLLOW ME" THE MASTER CALLED
"JUST TAKE A STEP, HOWEVER SMALL
DON'T BE AFRAID, I'LL BE RIGHT HERE
TO CATCH YOU WHEN YOU FALL!"

"Follow me..."
(Jesus in Matthew 4:19)

It had started off like any other shift. Peter and his brother, Andrew, headed to the beach and climbed into their boat hoping for a good catch. Fishing was unpredictable, even for seasoned fisherman like these, and the pressure to come home with a haul was relentless. It was a simple enough equation:

Empty nets = empty bellies.

Their strong arms hauled the net back into the boat as they prayed for fish.

Nothing.

Frustrated but undeterred, they hurled the net back out, as they had done countless times before. It was a well-rehearsed routine that their father had drilled into them since childhood. The net splashed down into uncertain waters and again they prayed for fish.

A solitary, windswept figure watched them from the shore. They were vaguely aware of his gaze but paid no attention—they had more important things to be preoccupied with, namely, catching fish! But then the man on the shore called out to them—and that's when everything changed.

> *Follow me, and I will make you fishers of men.*
> *(Matthew 4:19)*

The voice was irresistible. It penetrated their hardened defences and took root in the soft, fertile soil of souls that were hungry, desperate even, to be part of something greater. This was more than a strange job offer, it was a sacred moment. A high call to a new life of divine purpose and eternal significance. They didn't need long to think about it: "Immediately they left their nets and followed him" (v 20).

Drawn by love and propelled by faith, Peter and Andrew responded to Jesus' call to "follow me" and in doing so became the first disciples to join Jesus on his mission to change the world. They were certainly not the last. For the last two millennia, innumerable men, women and children have heard the same voice issue the same invitation and joyfully leapt at the chance to leave their old lives and follow Jesus.

Including me.

What about you?

In this chapter we will start taking steps on our hopeward journey. We'll be helped on our way by a man who perhaps resonates with me more than anyone else in Scripture—Peter. In Matthew 4 Peter might have burst out of the blocks in passionate pursuit of Jesus, but eventually he crumples, just like the rest of us.

But while Peter is going to fail spectacularly, his failure will be matched—eclipsed, even—by the faithfulness of Jesus. It is my hope and prayer that as you see the way Jesus graciously deals with Peter, your faith will soar and you too will be moved to dust yourself down and start taking courageous steps of faith.

Ready?

1. TO FOLLOW JESUS IS TO WALK WITH HIM

Following Jesus is no walk in the park (excuse the pun). "Follow me" is a command that requires active, not passive, obedience. These new disciples didn't stay on the beach—they followed their roaming Rabbi wherever he went.

For the next three years, Jesus' small posse of disciples walked with him step-by-step from town to town and village to village: listening to his astonishing teaching, asking burning questions, marvelling at his miracles, observing his love for the outcast, and watching with wide eyes and open mouths as he confounded religious leaders.

Walking with Jesus was a learning experience. The disciples learned how to love, how to pray, how to understand the Scriptures, how to serve, how to sacrifice and how to see people as God sees them.

This was no spectator sport: it required participation. Jesus would send his disciples out to perform various tasks and errands. They went "like lambs among wolves" to pray, preach and heal the sick (Luke 10:3, NIV). And sure, it might have been Jesus who blessed the packed lunch that fed 5,000 hungry mouths, but it was the disciples who got to dish it all out (and tidy up afterwards)!

This active participation in the ministry of Jesus is not limited to those who were following him in the flesh in the first century. Check out what Jesus said to his disciples in John 14:12 (my emphasis):

> *Truly, truly, I say to you, **whoever** believes in me will also do the works that I do; and greater works than these will he do, because I am going to the Father.*

Even today, those who believe in Jesus are called to carry on walking in his ways—sacrificially loving and serving others, faithfully praying, clinging to God's word and holding it out to others. Another of Jesus' disciples, John, put it this way: "Whoever says he abides in [Jesus] ought to walk in the same way in which he walked" (1 John 2:6). In other words, we are to continue what Jesus started in this world by continuing to walk his way.

The Bible provides us with multiple references to what walking with Jesus involves. We are called to:

- walk in love (Ephesians 5:2).

- walk in the light (John 8:12).

- walk fearlessly (Psalm 23:4).

- walk by the Spirit (Galatians 5:16).

- walk in newness of life (Romans 6:4).

- walk humbly with our God (Micah 6:8).

- walk by faith and not by sight (2 Corinthians 5:7).

- walk in the good works that God has prepared for us (Ephesians 2:10).

Quite a challenging list, eh?

At this point, the temptation for those of us who still feel weak might be to ask if we can get a pass. But if we are going to keep heading hopeward, we have to push through that pain barrier.

Many moons ago I was a fearless but foolish skateboarder. (My signature trick was ending up in hospital!) Consequently, I have a lengthy list of broken body parts. Possibly the most painful injury I suffered was a torn ACL that required reconstructive surgery.

In the days following the operation all I wanted to do was watch movies and get high on morphine! I used to dread the physio coming onto the ward each morning to get me out of bed and back onto my feet. I can still hear her voice now: *"I know it hurts but it's vital that you start moving it now, otherwise you may never get your full range of motion back"*.

I kind of hated her for saying it even though I knew that it was true. I had to get moving again. Each day I would crawl off my hospital bed, stand gingerly to my feet, grab my crutches and try to follow her off the ward and down the corridor. It hurt so much.

Every.

Single.

Step.

But I knew I had to do it.

Dear friend, at the risk of sounding like my old physio— it's time to get back on your feet. I know that sounds scary and you might not feel ready, but there is a whole load of beautiful stuff that Jesus has still got for you to do.

Perhaps you already know exactly what it is that Jesus wants you to be doing, but such is your brokenness right now that you cannot envisage *ever* being able to accomplish it. The shame of that only compounds the misery. Or perhaps you have absolutely no idea what God could possibly want to do in and through you, such is your sense of inadequacy.

Whatever doubts and fears you might be wrestling with right now, I want to encourage you with this profound truth: Jesus has not walked away from you. He still wants to walk with you. And don't worry—he's going to be with you every step of the way, as we're about to learn from Peter.

2. JESUS WILL CATCH US WHEN WE FALL

One of the things I love about Peter is that he was one of those all-or-nothing disciples. A perfect example of this is the time when, after being initially spooked by Jesus walking on the waves in the midst of a storm, Peter decided to climb out of the boat and try the same thing. Incredibly, one trembling, squelching step after another, he actually does it! Peter starts walking on water...

> *But when he saw the wind, he was afraid, and beginning to sink he cried out, "Lord, save me." Jesus immediately reached out his hand and took hold of him, saying to him, "O you of little faith, why did you doubt?" And when they got into the boat, the wind ceased. And those in the boat worshipped him, saying, "Truly you are the Son of God." (Matthew 14:30-33)*

Peter took his eyes off Jesus and his faith was quickly evicted by fear. He cried out as he started to sink—and Jesus was right there to catch him!

Did Peter doubt? Yes.

Did his faith fail? Yes.

Did Jesus fail? No!

Here's what this tells us:

- Jesus' strength is greater than our weakness.

- He is faithful even when we are faithless.

- He *will* catch us when we fall.

I don't know about you, but for me this is *so* reassuring. One of the great barriers to getting back on our feet and starting to follow Jesus again is the fear of falling. That was certainly true for me when I crumpled a few years ago. My church graciously gave me some time out to recover, but those first few steps back into life and ministry were, frankly, terrifying. What if I go down again?

Jesus' faithful hold on Peter gave me great courage and confidence to take those steps. How wonderful to know that Jesus will reach out and grab us when our faith falters and we start to sink.

And this would not be the last time that Jesus would have to reach out and rescue a floundering Peter. Let's fast forward to Peter's worst day ever, or as I like to call it, Cockerelgate!

3. THERE IS GRACE FOR EVERY FALTERING FOOTSTEP

As the shadow of the cross loomed darker and larger over the latter days of Jesus' life, he spoke openly about the betrayal and suffering that he was about to face. Shortly after his last supper with them Jesus told his disciples, "You will all fall away, for it is written, 'I will strike the shepherd, and the sheep will be scattered'" (Mark 14:27).

Peter, cocky as ever, fired back, "Even though they all fall away, *I will not*" (v 29, my emphasis).

But Jesus knew better: "Truly, I tell you, this very night, before the cock crows twice, you will deny me three times" (v 30).

Undeterred, Peter doubled down: "If I must die with you, *I will not deny you*" (v 31, my emphasis).

You've got to love Peter! Such bold promises, no doubt born out of sincere love for Jesus, but so foolishly built on the shaky foundations of his own strength and resolve.

Most of us know how the story goes from here—Jesus is betrayed by Judas, his disciples flee (yes, even Peter) and Jesus is dragged before a kangaroo court at the home of the high priest. Poignantly, Matthew, Mark and Luke all record that Peter followed him all the way into the high priest's courtyard, but that he "followed him *at a distance*" (Mark 14:54).

I find that distance so unsettling. This same Peter who had immediately left everything to follow Jesus, who had even jumped out of a ship in a storm to follow Jesus, was now following at a distance. A gap had opened up between Peter and his beloved Lord.

Can you relate to that?

It gets worse. Some of those in the courtyard with Peter recognise him and start to press him on his connection to Jesus. He twice denies knowing Jesus. Then a cockerel crows. He curses and denies Jesus a third time. And then "immediately the cock crowed a second time. And Peter remembered how Jesus had said to him, 'Before the cock crows twice, you will deny me three times.' And he broke down and wept" (Mark 14:72).

Is this not one of the most agonising moments in all the Gospels? It's harrowing to see Peter mess up so spectacularly. So publicly. You can almost feel his heart breaking and his body juddering as bitter tears of shame batter the dust of the courtyard floor.

He had such high hopes, he made such bold promises, and he failed so miserably—it's little wonder that Peter broke down.

He crumpled.

A short while later Jesus was sentenced to death by crucifixion. He was stripped, spat upon, mocked and beaten to within an inch of his life, then led to "the Place of the Skull", where he was nailed to a cross of wood and suspended between heaven and earth to die. Here, Jesus paid the penalty for *all* the sins of *all* his people, including Peter and including us.

Peter, however, was nowhere to be seen. Where was he?

Hiding.

    Cowering.

        Despairing.

            Still broken.

                Sound familiar?

How kind, then, that after Jesus rose from death three days later, his angel gave the following message to some courageous women outside his empty tomb:

> *Do not be alarmed. You seek Jesus of Nazareth, who was crucified. He has risen; he is not here. See the place where they laid him. But go, tell his disciples **and Peter** that he is going before you to Galilee. There you will see him, just as he told you.*
> *(Mark 16:6-7, my emphasis)*

Why did the angel specifically mention Peter by name? Perhaps because the resurrected Jesus had a huge dollop of restorative grace that was just for him!

Sure enough, Jesus appeared several times to his disciples in Galilee, but there is one particular encounter that I want us to focus on. Here's how it went down:

When they had finished breakfast, Jesus said to Simon Peter, "Simon, son of John, do you love me more than these?" He said to him, "Yes, Lord; you know that I love you." He said to him, "Feed my lambs."

He said to him a second time, "Simon, son of John, do you love me?" He said to him, "Yes, Lord; you know that I love you." He said to him, "Tend my sheep."

He said to him the third time, "Simon, son of John, do you love me?" Peter was grieved because he said to him the third time, "Do you love me?" and he said to him, "Lord, you know everything; you know that I love you."

Jesus said to him, "Feed my sheep. Truly, truly, I say to you, when you were young, you used to dress yourself and walk wherever you wanted, but when you are old, you will stretch out your hands, and another will dress you and carry you where you do not want to go." (This he said to show by what kind of death he was to glorify God.)

And after saying this he said to him, "Follow me."
(John 21:15-19)

So many things can be gleaned from these verses, but I want to draw your attention to just two:

1. JESUS STILL HAD WORK FOR PETER TO DO

Yes, Peter had failed, but Jesus had not finished with him yet. There were sheep and lambs that needed to be cared for and Peter was the shepherd that Jesus wanted for the job. (And the book of Acts shows us that Peter did indeed get back on his feet and get on with it!)

And Jesus still has work for us to do too. Ephesians 2:10 tells us that "we are his workmanship, created in Christ Jesus for good works, which God prepared beforehand, that we should walk in them".

Read those words again and ask God to help you take them to heart. If God has gone to the trouble of saving us, shaping us and creating us for *specific* good works, prepared for us long before we ever messed it all up, let's not think for a minute that our crumpling can somehow nullify all that. No way! It's God's grace, not our failure, that has the last word over our lives. There are still good works for us to walk in and, mercifully, there is grace for every faltering footstep.

2. THE CALL ON PETER'S LIFE HADN'T CHANGED

Read those last two words again. "Follow me." Same beach. Same fisherman. Same Saviour. Same invitation. A coincidence? Surely not! Peter had fallen hard, but Jesus hadn't changed his mind about him.

Jesus' words to Peter are evidence that a calamitous history of disobedience and disgrace is not enough to dampen God's love or make him change his mind about us. He still wanted to walk with Peter. And he still wants to walk with us.

Jesus has more grace than we have disgrace.

More patience than we have capitulations.

More faithfulness than we have faithlessness.

More mercy than we have mess.

More good works for us still to do.

Jesus was under absolutely no illusions about Peter when he first called him from the shore of the Sea of Galilee, and he's under no illusions about us either. He knew Peter would falter. He knew we would too. But Jesus wasn't finished with Peter, and he isn't finished with us. Like Peter, he still wants us to follow him hopeward—to walk out the beauty of his gospel with footsteps of faith in our fallen, fractured world.

So, whatever it is that has crumpled you, crippled you and kept you down, I'm pretty sure I know what Peter would want to say to you: "In the name of Jesus Christ of Nazareth, rise up and walk!" (Acts 3:6).

*Lord Jesus, thank you for the honour of being called
to follow you. I'm sorry that because of my own
sin, the sins of others and the struggles of life, I so
often fail and fall. I am grateful for the grace that
you make available to stumbling saints like me.
Thank you that you knew how this was going to go
long before you called me and that you have been so
patient and gracious ever since. Thank you for dying
in my place, to take away all my sin. Forgive me, I
pray. Thank you that there are still good works that
you have for me to do. Please strengthen me and
walk with me as I seek to faithfully follow you. Amen*

REFLECTION QUESTIONS

1. Which aspects of Peter's journey (his passionate pursuit / epic failure / gracious restoration) do you relate to, and how?

2. How do you feel about stepping out in courageous faith and walking with Jesus again? What specific fears are holding you back? Talk to God about them now.

3. What "good works" might Jesus have for you to do in the weeks, months and years ahead?

7. RUN TO JESUS
(Run the race with endurance)

SO PRESS ON, WEARY SOUL
ROARED ON BY SAINTS OF OLD
FIX YOUR EYES ON CHRIST THE PRIZE
KEEP RUNNING
HOPEWARD
HOME.

The Bible uses many analogies to describe the Christian life, but one of the most prominent is that of a race. I have to confess that I feel like a bit of an imposter writing about running because I've never been any good at it. (Although it's worth mentioning that I did win the obstacle race in primary school. Twice!) But here, on the last leg of our hopeward journey, we have to run—and run competitively:

> *Do you not know that in a race all the runners run, but only one receives the prize? So run that you may obtain it. (1 Corinthians 9:24)*

While there are certain similarities between walking (the last chapter) and running (this chapter), the main thing we need to focus on here is the race component—the idea that there is a course marked out, a rapturous crowd watching and the promise of a prize when we cross the finish line.

However, I can already hear some of you mumbling under your breath as you tentatively reach for your running shoes:

- I don't even know if I can do this!

- What if I stumble and fall again?

- What if I end up right back where I started?

I hear you. It's exhausting just thinking about running for Jesus. However, there is help, hope and astonishing grace available to us. Let's reflect on some wonderful words written to reassure reluctant runners and apprehensive athletes like us:

> *Therefore, since we are surrounded by so great a cloud of witnesses, let us also lay aside every weight, and sin which clings so closely, and let us run with endurance the race that is set before us, looking to Jesus, the founder and perfecter of our faith, who for the joy that was set before him endured the cross, despising the shame, and is seated at the right hand of the throne of God. (Hebrews 12:1-2)*

1. LOOK AROUND

This passage comes hot on the heels of Hebrews 11: a mighty chapter that serves as something of a "Hall of Fame" of the Bible's faith heroes. It's well worth a read—right now if you have time.

Some of their exploits are simply jaw-dropping: swerving death and going straight to heaven (Enoch); preserving the human race *and* the animal kingdom (Noah); bearing miracle babies in old age (Sarah); leading a whole nation out of slavery through the Red Sea (Moses). Not to mention the ones towards the end of the list "who through faith conquered kingdoms, enforced justice, obtained promises, stopped the mouths of lions, quenched the power of fire, escaped the edge of the sword, were made strong out of weakness, became mighty in war, put foreign armies to flight" (v 33-34).

Pretty intimidating to mere mortals like us, though, right?! I mean, I look around at these names and I feel like a toddler in the presence of Olympic legend Mo Farah! It only feels like two minutes ago that I was face down in the dust, unable to face life anymore—and now I'm meant to get out there and "compete" like that?!

But here's the thing: if that's how we see these saints then we are looking at them the wrong way. When we look more closely at this "cloud of witnesses" we see that we are surrounded by failures! They are men and women who had moments, even seasons, when they crumpled, just like us:

- Ever felt like drinking yourself into oblivion? Noah has.

- Ever sold someone out to save your own skin? Abraham has.

- Ever mocked God? Sarah has.

- Ever wrestled with God... and limped ever since? Jacob has.

- Ever known the agony of a broken home and the rejection of a family? Joseph has.

- Ever given God a list of excuses for why you can't serve him? Moses has.

- Ever wondered if God can still use you despite your shameful past? Rahab has.

- Ever felt too small, weak and insignificant for the task? Gideon has.

- Ever let your sex-drive lead you into catastrophic sin? Samson has.

- Ever felt utterly crushed by guilt for wrongs that you can never put right? David has.

Yes, these men and women may be lauded as heroes of the faith, but they are not the ones we should ultimately be looking to. It was the object of their faith, Jesus, who made the difference. *He* is the only reason they finished the race. They are not standing in the crowd, pointing at themselves shouting "look at us". Rather they are pointing at Jesus emphatically screaming, "Look at him!"

So don't look around and see men and women that you could never emulate in your wildest dreams. Look instead at the kind of wasters, losers, sinners and scumbags that God graciously allows to run for him, and be encouraged that if *they* made it across the finish line, then so can we!

2. LAY ASIDE

With this gallery of inglorious forerunners very much in view, the author then calls us to action. We are not here to spectate but to participate:

> *Therefore, since we are surrounded by so great a cloud of witnesses, **let us also lay aside every weight, and sin which clings so closely,** and let us run with endurance the race that is set before us...*
> *(Hebrews 12:1, my emphasis)*

There is a race that has already been set for us to run. I hope that this in itself is an encouragement—that God has a plan and a path already marked out for us and all that we have been through thus far has not altered the route. However, if we are going to get back on track and start running for the prize again, there are some things we need to offload: namely, the burdens that crush us and the sins that cling to us.

CRUSHING BURDENS

When athletes compete, they wear the lightest and most streamlined clothing available. The idea of "weight" here conjures up an image of someone instead trying to run a marathon with a backpack loaded with bricks!

The very first stage of our journey together involved responding to Jesus' offer to come to him and let him bear our burdens. It was an invitation that we simply could not refuse, and we gladly laid them all down. Yet here we are limbering up trackside, aware that somewhere along the way we may have picked up some of that old baggage again—fear, frustration, doubt, insecurity, old habits...

What's wrong with us?!

The things that can weigh us down are many and varied. Perhaps one of the most problematic (and exhausting) burdens that we all too often return to is our addiction to legalistic attitudes. This shows itself in obsessing over keeping rules (and keeping score), doing things to look good to others, and heaping judgement on those who don't measure up to our standards.

The Galatian churches were certainly guilty of this when they chose slavish obedience to the Old Testament's law over the freedom that was theirs in Christ:

> *O foolish Galatians! Who has bewitched you? ... You*
> *were running well. Who hindered you?*
> *(Galatians 3:1; 5:7)*

The religious can't run for long because the weight of trying to prove themselves, either to God or to other people, is both unbearable and unsustainable. Legalism will always squash the life out of us eventually, because none of us have the strength or the virtue to save ourselves. This is why the ministry of Jesus is so liberating. Jesus lived the perfect life that we never could have and died the sinner's death that we really should have. To know Jesus is to be liberated from the crushing, suffocating pressure of religion.

Take a moment to breathe that in and let freedom fill your lungs.

SIN WHICH CLINGS

The weight of legalism is not our only problem, however. Equally unhelpful is sin "which clings so closely". I have strong childhood memories of my green-fingered father despairing in the garden because he couldn't get rid of what he called "flicky weeds" (commonly known as "cleavers"). These are weeds that stick to anything and everything. They cling to your clothes like a tantruming child but also latch on to healthy plants and choke the life out of those too. They are an absolute nightmare to get rid of.

A bit like stubborn sin that...

Just.

Wont.

Let.

Go!

It frustrates me intensely that 30 years into this race I am still stumbling over the same old sins (and finding new ones to trip on too!). Lifelong vices, shameful habits and murky mindsets still have their claws sunk into me and continue to haul me back and drag me down.

Is that your experience too?

If we are going to run this race with endurance, then we need to get shot of our burdens and jettison our sin.

In John Bunyan's classic story, *The Pilgrim's Progress*, there is a beautiful moment when Christian finally arrives at the cross of Jesus and the heavy load that had been weighing him down for so long finally drops from his back and rolls down into the grave. Christian, we are told, gives three leaps for joy and then breaks out in song:

Thus far did I come laden with my sin,
Nor could aught ease the grief that I was in,
Till I came hither. What a place is this!
Must here be the beginning of my bliss!
Must here the burden fall from off my back!
Must here the strings that bound it to me crack!
Blest cross! Blest sepulchre! Blest rather be
The Man that there was put to shame for me!

Christian learned, as we need to, that the only one who can deal with the weight that would crush us and the sin that would strangle us is The Man—Jesus! He was there at the start of this hopeward adventure, and he has been patiently, faithfully walking alongside us this whole time. So it should come as no surprise that he is the one to whom we must continually come if we are to rid ourselves of besetting sin, and he is the one to whom we must keep looking if we are going to reach that finish line.

How do we ditch our sack full of sin? We get on our knees and confess it in prayer: "If we confess our sins, he is faithful and just to forgive us our sins and to cleanse us from all unrighteousness" (1 John 1:9).

3. LOOK TO JESUS

Let's end our time together in the same way as we started—looking to Jesus! What do we see that could strengthen our hearts, energise our faith and put a fresh spring in our step? Let's specifically consider who Jesus is, what he did and where he is:

> ... *looking to Jesus, the founder and perfecter of our faith, who for the joy that was set before him endured the cross, despising the shame, and is seated at the right hand of the throne of God. (Hebrews 12:2)*

WHO HE IS: FOUNDER AND PERFECTER OF OUR FAITH

Jesus is the "founder" of our faith. The NIV translates this word as "pioneer". The KJV uses "author". All of these words are helpful because they describe Jesus as the one who has gone ahead of us, beating a track for us to follow.

We have not been left to chart this course alone. Our pioneer knows first-hand how to navigate every single obstacle that we could ever face. Our author holds the pen and has written the script for our lives—even the tough bits. We have no need to fear whatever the next chapter may hold. We can trust him to write a story for our lives that is glorious, marked by grace, and that ultimately has a happy ending—the salvation of our souls (see 1 Peter 1:9).

But there's more. Jesus is also the "perfecter" (ESV) or "finisher" (KJV) of our faith. What does that mean?

Let's go back to the 1992 Barcelona Olympics to find out. It's the men's 400m semi-final, and running for Team GB is a sprinter called Derek Redmond, the reigning British record holder. The starting pistol cracks and Redmond is off to a great start.

However, as he comes out of the first bend, his hamstring pops and he collapses to the track clutching his leg in agony. Astonishingly, he gets back to his feet, determined to finish the race—though it's immediately clear that the pain is unbearable.

It is at this point that his father, Jim, bursts past security staff, runs to his son, and puts his arm around him to support him. Through floods of tears, Derek says: "Dad, I want to finish, get me back in the semi-final". To which Jim replies: "Ok. We started this thing together and now we'll finish it together" (https://www.awesomestories. com/pdf/make/155463).

The image of Jim helping his son to finish the race, waving away every official who tries to stop him, is one of the most iconic Olympic images of all time. As they cross the finish line 65,000 rapturous fans stand to their feet and roar him home.

As followers of Jesus, we might feel like we have crashed too hard to ever make it back. But when we look through our tears to the founder *and* finisher of our faith, it's as if he rushes to us and reassures us: *We started this thing together and now we'll finish it together*. Paul shared this confidence:

> *I am sure of this, that he who began a good work in you will bring it to completion at the day of Jesus Christ. (Philippians 1:6)*

Brothers and sisters, we're gonna make it, because of Jesus!

WHAT HE DID: JOYFULLY ENDURED THE CROSS

The second thing that encourages us as we look to Jesus is what he did—and why. Jesus endured the cross, refusing to wilt under its shame.

Why?

Hebrews 12 tells us it was because of the epic "joy" that awaited him on the other side (v 2).

And what joy was that?

The bliss of being home with the Father in heaven? Yes.

The satisfaction of knowing that he had completed his mission? For sure.

However, I believe that the joy foremost in the mind of Jesus as he hung on the cross was the joy of "seeing" all those who would be rescued and made right with God through his death. Check out what Isaiah prophesied about Jesus:

> *Out of the anguish of his soul he shall **see** and be satisfied;*
> *by his knowledge shall the righteous one, my servant,*
> *make many to be accounted righteous,*
> *and he shall bear their iniquities.*
> *(Isaiah 53:11, my emphasis)*

In the midst of the horror and excruciating anguish of the cross, the suffering servant saw heaven being populated by a grace-saved multitude. As Jesus hung beneath a blackened sky, suspended between a holy heaven and a wicked world, he knew that the very blood pouring from his wounds and trickling down the cross was the means by which rebels would be reconciled to God, sinners would become saints and the filthy would be washed clean.

Jesus did not die grudgingly for us.

He died gladly for us.

Because he loves us.

He really does!

Jesus endured the cross for the joy of redeeming us. As we look to him, may the joy of that redemption help us to endure for him.

WHERE HE IS: ENTHRONED IN HEAVEN

Finally, let's lift our eyes together to where Jesus is now. Having come as a servant, died as our substitute and risen as our Saviour, Jesus ascended back to where he truly belongs—"seated at the right hand of the throne of God" (Hebrews 12:2).

This is *such* good news for us. Both the posture and the position of Christ are significant here. Firstly, he is seated. He is sat down because, as the hymnwriter Charles Wesley put it, "Love's redeeming work is done".

Jesus cried, "It is finished" from the cross (John 19:30), because it is! Our debt has been cancelled, our freedom has been secured and our adoption papers have been signed. There is nothing left to pay and nothing left to prove. Jesus finished the race before us and has blazed a trail for us to follow.

Hallelujah!

Secondly, Jesus is sat *at the Father's right hand*—the place of highest honour and greatest glory. No one has more power and authority than the undefeated, undisputed champion of heaven.

If the King of kings, Lord of lords and conqueror of death is for us, who the dickens can be against us? And how amazing to think that *right now* Jesus is sat at the right hand of the Father praying for us: "Christ Jesus is the one who died—more than that, who was raised—who is at the right hand of God, who indeed is interceding for us" (Romans 8:34).

"Interceding" is the act of standing in the gap on behalf of someone else and pleading on their behalf. That's what Jesus is doing for you. Imagine him leaning into the Father and whispering:

> *Father, I am burdened for [your name]. They are really struggling right now. Could you reach into your abundant resources of grace and grant them all that they stand in need of? Please strengthen, encourage and sustain them, Father, until they make it safely home to us!*

That would change things, right? It certainly did for the minister Robert Murray M'Cheyne: "If I could hear Christ praying for me in the next room, I would not fear a million enemies. Yet distance makes no difference. He is praying for me."

PREPARED FOR US

Friends, we're running—and we're running home. But we're not home yet. The race marked out for us meanders through hostile foreign territory. We are pilgrims passing through a barren land. However, as we struggle for Jesus *down here*, we can be encouraged that he is doing beautiful things for us *up there*.

> *Let not your hearts be troubled. Believe in God; believe also in me. In my Father's house are many rooms. If it were not so, would I have told you that I go to prepare a place for you? And if I go and prepare a place for you, I will come again and will take you to myself, that where I am you may be also.*
>
> *(John 14:1-3)*

We don't belong down here; we belong up there with him. When the race feels impossible and the finish line too far away, is there a sweeter thought to ponder than that of Jesus personally preparing our room for us in heaven?

He knows how many times we crumpled and capitulated.

He is fully familiar with our history of failure and shame.

And *still* he loves us and wants us with him.

For ever.

He's getting things ready to receive us *right now!*

Wow!

That, friends, is why we should keep looking to Jesus and Jesus *alone*. Through the pain and the shame. The doubts and the fears. The trials and the tears. When we feel like we can't take...

One.

More.

Step.

In these moments it's crucial that we fix our eyes on the one who finished the race ahead of us, who right now sits at the right of the Father, who is praying for our perseverance, preparing a place for us in paradise, and who will one day rise from his throne to split the sky and take us home to a place where we will *never* sin, struggle, cry or crumple again. This is the prize that we are running to lay hold of.

This is how it will end for every true follower of Jesus— the glorious crescendo of the hopeward trajectory.

So to my fellow strugglers and stragglers, limping sheep and crumpled heaps, in light of all that we've learned on our journey together...

Let's look to Jesus.

And let's run to him.

Onward.

Hopeward.

Until we're home.

Lord Jesus, I have known such weakness, such exhaustion and such failure that the thought of running this race is hard to comprehend. But I thank you that you completed the race ahead of me and even now you are rooting for me, praying for me and waiting for me at the finish line. It feels so far away, and my legs still feel like they could buckle at any moment. Lord Jesus, I love you. This is all for you. Please help me to keep looking to you. Strengthen me and grant me supernatural endurance. Keep me to the end I pray. For your glory. Amen.

REFLECTION QUESTIONS

1. What burdens are still weighing you down and what sins are still clinging to you? Imagine bringing them to the cross of Jesus and laying them down at its foot.

2. How does looking at the person and work of Jesus energise your strides and encourage your heart as you run to him?

3. What is most exhilarating to you about the thought of crossing that finish line and making it "home"?

CLOSING WORDS

I'm sat here alone in my living room on a fresh winter's morning. The house is completely empty apart from two dopey dogs dozing deliriously in the shards of sunlight streaming through the window. Flames dance playfully around the log burner and I've just washed down a sumptuous slice of Victoria sponge cake with a perfect, velvety coffee. Lush.

As I set to typing out these closing words in this idyllic scene my mind is clear, my faith is strong and my heart is happy and hopeful. And it all feels quite surreal. As I read back through all that I've written over the last few years (yes, it has taken that long) I feel *really* emotional.

I am still the same man who lay flat on his back staring helplessly at the ceiling in chapter 1, and yet I'm also very different now. In some ways, it feels like that all happened yesterday, and yet in other ways it feels like a lifetime ago. As God has graciously helped me to keep stumbling hopeward, I feel grateful beyond words that my crumpling was neither the defining nor the concluding moment of my life. There was sweet, timely gospel grace for my weary soul, and I will be eternally thankful to him for that.

Even so, I live with this overwhelming, sobering awareness that I haven't crossed that finish line. Yet. Part of the process of writing this book has been learning more about myself with the help of my family, my church, trusted friends and mental health professionals. It's been humbling. I feel far more stable and far more hopeful than I have done for many years. But at the same time, I still feel vulnerable to some of the same lies and besetting weaknesses that brought me down last time. I wish that wasn't the case, but it is.

I share this because I know that there is every chance that you have reached this point in the book and feel the same—hopeful yet fearful. If that's the case, dear brother or sister, I want to end our time together by reminding you of some of the gospel truths that I have sought to weave throughout the pages of this book. These are truths that I fight to cling to daily for the sake of my own soul. It is my sincere prayer that they will serve you well also.

First, your failure is not final. It wasn't last time and won't be next time.

Second, should you fail again, your Redeemer will not forsake you. He will pursue you just as passionately. He will call you just as gently. He will hold out his grace just as freely. And he will embrace you just as warmly. His love for you has not dwindled and it never will.

Third, his gospel has lost none of its power. Forgiveness, freedom, healing and transformational power are yours for ever in Christ. You don't just need to know these truths to become a Christian—you need them to fill you up and sustain you on every day that follows. Seek to feast on this gospel daily for the rest of your life.

Fourth, God's desire is for you to grow in the strength of his love. That remains steadfast. Even now, the Holy Spirit is at work in your life to strengthen and encourage you. Furthermore, the church remains the primary means by which God wants you to grow, and help others to grow, in faith, hope and love.

Finally, Jesus has not given up on you and he never will. He will walk faithfully with you and he will catch you when you fall. Every. Single. Time. So run the race with your eyes fixed on him and keep heading hopeward and homeward all the way to the very end.

Come.

Receive.

Abide.

Feast.

Grow.

Walk.

Run.

And repeat as many times as necessary until *that* day when you cross the finish line and crumple one final time at the feet of Jesus, not in exhaustion, but in worship. Not as a failure, but as a victor.

Never to struggle again.

Never to break again.

Never to weep again.

Never to sin again.

Home with him.

For ever.

> *May the God of hope fill you with all joy and peace in believing, so that by the power of the Holy Spirit you may abound in hope. (Romans 15:13)*

HOPEWARD

I LAY IN A CRUMPLED HEAP
NOT STRONG, BUT WEAK
A PITIFUL MESS BUT BLESSED
TO COLLAPSE AT THE MASTER'S FEET.

MY TROUBLED SOUL WAS WEARY
MY HEART WAS COLD AND HEAVY
"COME, RECEIVE MY REST"
HE WHISPERED TO ME GENTLY.

HIS WORDS WERE KIND AND TRUE:
"I KNOW WHAT YOU'VE BEEN THROUGH.
I'VE GOT ALL THE GRACE YOU NEED
AND I'M GIVING IT TO YOU."

SUCH MERCY IN HIS FACE
AS HE LAVISHED ME WITH GRACE
MY WEARY SOUL FOUND REST
IN THE WARMTH OF HIS EMBRACE.

I FEASTED ON HIS GOSPEL
AND WHERE BEFORE I'D CRUMPLED
FRESH STRENGTH BEGAN TO RISE
AS HOPEWARD FAITH WAS KINDLED.

EMBOLDENED BY THE SAINTS
EMPOWERED BY THE SPIRIT
I BEGAN TO GRASP THE LOVE OF CHRIST —
A LOVE THAT KNOWS NO LIMITS.

DAI HANKEY

"FOLLOW ME" THE MASTER CALLED
"JUST TAKE A STEP, HOWEVER SMALL
DON'T BE AFRAID, I'LL BE RIGHT HERE
TO CATCH YOU WHEN YOU FALL!"

SO PRESS ON, WEARY SOUL
ROARED ON BY SAINTS OF OLD
FIX YOUR EYES ON CHRIST THE PRIZE
KEEP RUNNING
HOPEWARD
HOME.